The Mystical Year

The Mystical Year

By the Editors of Time-Life Books

TIME-LIFE BOOKS, ALEXANDRIA, VIRGINIA

CONTENTS

Captured at a moment of total eclipse in the photograph at left, earth's nearest star appears no more than a static nimbus of spark and flame. But no heavenly object influences life on our planet more than does the sun. As the hemispheres of earth tilt toward it and away, the changing amounts of light they receive shape four familiar seasons: Warming spring gives way to summer, then dusky fall, and—finally—killing winter. To some philosophers, the seasons mirror the birth, youth, adulthood, and senescence of humankind. To others, the return of spring is the surest sign that the cycle of life never ends.

In the pages that follow, the days of the solar year—365 plus one for the quadrennial leap year that keeps the calendar synchronized with the sun—are celebrated with an abundance of mystical rites and mysterious occurrences, ranging from seasonal ghosts and demons to odd premonitions, extraplanetary visits, and time-honored rituals. Some are associated with particular dates. Others take place according to the phases of the moon and are shown on a day within the range of Western dates upon which they may fall.

Another class of anniversaries, perhaps the most mystical of all, is by necessity omitted from this calendar—each reader's own birthday. A birthday is richly endowed with meaning by astrologers, numerologists, and tradition. It is a personal New Year's Day and will evoke in each individual the New Year impulse to review the past and contemplate the meaning of the years to come.

S pring sunlight pouring through a stairway of the Castillo, a thousand-year-old pyramid at the Chichén Itzá ruins in Mexico, creates the shadow image of a serpent, an ancient Mayan symbol of rebirth and renewal. The sinuous pattern appears on the pyramid only twice a year, at sunset on spring and autumn equinoxes.

Old Solar Calendars of Stone

More than 5,000 years ago, centuries before the Pyramids rose above Egypt's sands, a tribe of Neolithic Irish farmers built a massive burial mound that still stands on a low ridge above the river Boyne. Deep inside, at the end of a sixty-two-foot-long stone passage, is the chamber where the dead were laid. For most of the year no light penetrates this sanctuary. But on a few mornings each winter, when the days are shortest and darkest, a shaft of sunlight enters a small opening above the tomb's entrance and beams straight down the long passageway *(page 15)*. For a few breathtaking moments, light fills the burial chamber, revealing a Stone Age cathedral of high vaulted ceilings and fancifully carved walls.

The dramatic illumination of Newgrange, as the tomb is called, occurs only in the few days around the winter solstice, when the sun reverses its retreat from the Northern Hemisphere and the days begin to lengthen. Scholars believe the creators of Newgrange laid out its more than 200,000 tons of stone deliberately to exploit the sun's position at this turning point in the solar year. If so, then these prehistoric architects were among the earliest humans to exhibit reverence for the celestial calendar by designing a structure in a precise astronomical relationship with the sun.

Ancient peoples watched the stars and planets closely, looking to the skies in search of order and meaning. The sun held particular prominence, revered both as the source of light and warmth and because its cyclical wanderings across the horizon provided reliable patterns of time and made nature predictable. Based on their observations, people divided the calendar into four seasons. Each centered on one of the four key dates that mark the sun's annual travels: the summer and winter solstices, which are respectively the year's longest and shortest days (approximately June 22 and December 22 in the Northern Hemisphere), and the spring and fall equinoxes, the two times of the year when the sun crosses the equator, making day and night equal in length (approximately March 21 and September 23).

Throughout history, humans have paid homage to the sun with special rites and festivals on these days. And many peoples, from the Maya who built the pyramid at left to the French churchmen, Chinese astronomers, American Indians, and others whose works are shown on the following pages, have created buildings specially designed to mark the dates. Cutting across barriers of time and culture, each of the structures is in itself a kind of sacred calendar, manifesting obeisance to the gods, the cycles of life and death, and the seasons of the mystical year.

*S*ummer's solstice sun cuts through the gloom of France's 800-year-old Chartres Cathedral and shines onto a large and mysteriously placed flagstone at the midpoint of the year's longest day.

Viewed from a solar temple that is located next to the great stone paws of Egypt's lionlike Sphinx, the sun at the summer solstice sets directly between the ancient pyramids of Cheops and Chephren.

From the center of the prehistoric stone rings of England's Stonehenge, the rising sun on the morning of the summer solstice appears almost directly above the tip of the Heel Stone, 256 feet away.

Fall's equinox is signaled when the shadow of a marker on top of this thirteenth-century Chinese solar observatory falls at midday on a particular spot on the long low measuring wall (foreground).

When viewed from the near end of this ball court in Mexico, which has been in continuous use since ancient Mayan times, the sun at the autumnal equinox sets precisely in the middle of the court's far end.

Winter sun shoots through an opening in the thousand-year-
old ruins of New Mexico's Pueblo Bonito on the morning of
the year's shortest day, and paints a far corner with light.

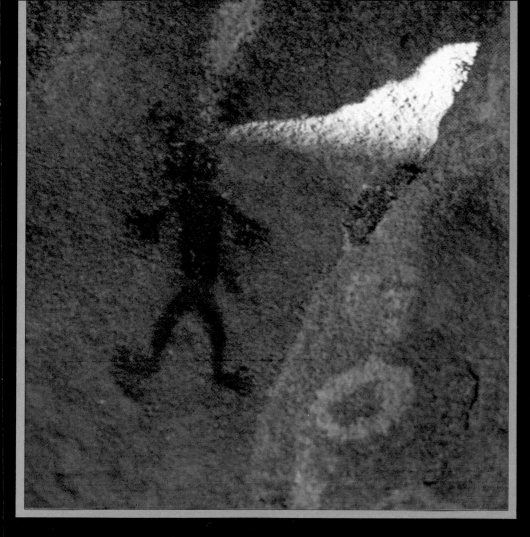

At sunrise on the winter solstice, a triangle of light pierces the eyes of a humanlike figure painted on the wall of an ancient Indian rock shelter in Mexico, giving it "sight."

Sun streams along the passage of Ireland's prehistoric Newgrange burial mound, lighting an interior that is dark except for the few days before and after the winter solstice.

The sun peeks above the horizon behind a natural sandstone marker in New Mexico's Chaco Canyon on December 22. For centuries on this day—the shortest of the year—Indians visited the spot to perform rituals asking the sun to return after the long winter nights.

Spring

March's talisman, the opaque red bloodstone, allegedly fortifies its wearer with courage, attracts fame, and ensures a long life.

The diamond is April's birthstone, and it is said to promote harmony between husband and wife—explaining its use in engagement rings.

May's birthstone, the emerald, is thought to bring good luck if worn in a garter. The precious green gem is also said to hasten the labor of a woman in childbirth.

Although the modern calendar begins the year in wintry January, most ancient cultures in the Northern Hemisphere marked the start of the annual cycle of existence with spring. The reason is self-evident. As March's promise and April's warming breath speed nature's pulse, human feeling and belief is swept along by an irresistible force—the surge of life itself. As illustrated in the following pages, the swirling emotional current of the season has inspired an extraordinary variety of spiritual rites and folk practices, but the overall direction is unmistakable: This is the season of revival and renewal. The northern face of the planet has tilted toward the sun (south of the equator, spring begins in September), and all living things respond—germinating, mating, reasserting strengths that had been held in check by the cold.

    The very names of the months attest to the quickening of the earth. March is named for Mars, primarily a god of war but also concerned with the fecundity of the soil. April's name derives from the Latin word *aperire,* "to open"—as blossoms do by the billion. May honors Maia, a Roman goddess who encouraged the growth of the crops.

    Since earliest times, societies have stepped back from the daily round to celebrate and assist the springing of life at this season. Many cultures have believed it necessary to help the transition from the old year to the new by supernatural means—by ceremonially killing a straw doll or other representation of winter, by banishing evil spirits, by ritually replacing old garments with new. Some societies have focused on propitiating gods of soil, water, rain, and sun so that plantings will flourish, a business that, in the past, often called for the sacrifice of animals, or even humans. But joy, too, has been used to supernaturally ensure fertility, exemplified by rollicking around a phallic maypole, by using eggs in rituals both pagan and Christian, and by joining in festivals that encourage shameless sexual frolics.

    Other large themes also shape the season. Some peoples choose this time to communicate with dead ancestors. Buddhists remind themselves with rites that the world is illusory, not real. But mostly spring's mystical aspect reflects its natural character. It is a time of release, a time of buoyant music and zestful dances—a time that all around the world is given over to the joy of being alive.

Resurgence of Life in Ancient Greece and Rome

For the ancient Greeks and Romans, the new year began not when the earth was chilled to its marrow but as life stirred again at the beginning of March. Both peoples celebrated the fresh start with symbolic actions.

In some parts of Greece, for example, a procession of children would escort February—represented by a lame man astride a donkey—out of the village in order to make way for March. Fires were ritually extinguished on the eve of the new year, and then relighted in the morning. Other customs, such as washing in the morning dew or sprinkling the members of a household with the first water drawn on that day, were thought to ensure good health.

Among the Romans, the first day of the new year was a time for celebrating and for exchanging gifts, including dates, figs, and honey—"that the year might in sweetness go through the course which it had begun," explained the poet Ovid. In addition, March 1 marked the Roman feast of Matronalia, the feminine counterpart of a winter festival for men called Saturnalia. On Matronalia, female slaves were allowed to abandon their duties for one day while their mistresses waited on them for a change.

As its name indicates, March was also sacred to Mars, the Roman god of war, whose birthday was celebrated along with the new year on the first, and whose praises were sung throughout the month. But the most important of religious rituals was the dousing of a sacred fire in the Temple of Vesta on the last day of February and its relighting on the first day of March. The ceremonies were conducted by the vestal virgins, official keepers of the flame. These six handmaids of Vesta, the goddess of the hearth, were picked for their job by the Pontifex Maximus, Rome's chief priest. Each girl was chosen before the onset of puberty and had to be the freeborn daughter of parents who were both living at the time. Each was required to remain a virgin for the entire length of her thirty-year term. To lose her virginity was to lose her life, traditionally by being buried alive.

1 MARCH

Granny March's Day. *In the Bulgarian language, March is the only month with a feminine name, and the calendar denotes its start as Granny March's Day. Throughout the country, women are admonished not to work on this date, lest they provoke the anger of Granny March and cause her to unleash a volley of storms that could destroy the crops.*

2 MARCH

A photo-snapping visitor? *On the evening of March 2, 1965, a man named John Reeves was strolling in the woods near his Florida home when he allegedly came upon a landed spacecraft with what appeared to be a robot wandering nearby. According to Reeves, the robot paused long enough to take his photograph, then boarded the vehicle and vanished into the sky. Searching the area, Reeves discovered two sheets of paper covered with unintelligible writing. The U.S. Air Force later investigated and pronounced the incident a hoax—a claim rejected by some ufologists.*

Chastely costumed in shapeless robes and a nunlike hood, this statue of a vestal virgin stands in the Forum at Rome. The Roman men were expected to heed the virgins' denial of sexuality, and any who did not were beaten to death.

A Day for Japanese Dolls and Girls

In Osaka, Japan, the people celebrate a thousand-year-old festival in which they make paper dolls and rub them on their bodies to draw off illnesses or evil spirits *(see July 25)*. A more widespread, modern doll festival, held on this day, involves borrowing the positive attributes of dolls instead of unloading negative ones onto them. Each Japanese girl creates a display of fifteen beautifully attired porcelain dolls—such as the one above—and shows them off to invited friends.

3 MARCH

Lost in the Triangle. *On March 3, 1918, the U.S. Navy vessel Cyclops steamed into the area of the Atlantic later dubbed the Bermuda Triangle. There she and her crew of 324 vanished without explanation.*

Greetings, aliens. *On this date in 1972, Pioneer 10 was launched into space, bearing an inscription (below) to tell anyone who encountered the craft where it came from and what its senders looked like.*

4 MARCH

Remembering the dead. *At about this time of year, ancient Greeks honored departed souls, or keres, with a three-day ritual called the Anthesteria, when the dead were believed to visit the living. At the conclusion of the rites, the spirits were dismissed with the words, ''Out, keres, the Anthesteria is ended.''*

5 MARCH

A saint's exploits. *This day marks the feast of Saint Ciaran, a sixth-century founder of Irish monasteries. Legend has it that when Ciaran was thirty years old, he traveled to Rome and met Saint Patrick, who later became the patron of Ireland. Patrick gave Ciaran a bell, asking him to take it to Ireland and build a monastery wherever the bell might toll of its own accord. One place the bell rang was called Saighir, and when Ciaran stopped there to build a home, four wild animals presented themselves. A wild boar, a wolf, a badger, and a fox offered help with the work and thus became Ciaran's first monks.*

6 MARCH

The priests of Mars. *On several dates during the month of March, a brotherhood of Roman warrior-priests known as the Salii danced in honor of the god Mars. Clad in what was, even then, old-fashioned Roman war dress, they leaped about wildly, brandishing spears and rhythmically beating their figure-eight shields, or ancilia. The original ancile was said to have been dropped from heaven by Mars as a sign that Rome was under the god's protection.*

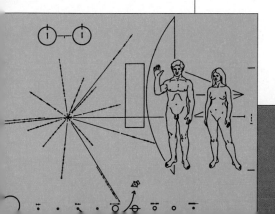

When Reality Melts Like Butter

At the heart of Buddhist belief is the idea that all worldly things are transient, destined to melt away in the current of time. On March 9, Tibetans act out this central truth during a festival that features Buddhist heroes made out of butter.

Monks begin to prepare for the so-called Butter Lamp Festival long beforehand by mixing bright dyes into tons of iced butter. Over a period of months, the butter is carved into elaborate effigies, some of them towering two stories high.

For the festival, the butter sculptures—mounted on wooden frames and gleaming in the light of lanterns—are paraded through streets packed with crowds of delighted onlookers. But the creamery heroes do not last for long. Following the procession, the monks who worked so hard to build them take their creations apart and heave the materials into a river, underscoring the key tenet of their faith.

A woman spoons yak butter into a lamp during the Tibetan Butter Lamp Festival. Faithful Tibetans believe the lamps strip demons of their power while securing the favor of the gods.

7 MARCH

A spirit photographer. *British carpenter William Hope, who died on this day in 1933, did not discover his alleged psychic gifts until he was forty-two years old. He and a friend were taking photographs of each other, when a plate that Hope exposed revealed the image of a weirdly transparent-looking woman, whom the friend recognized as his long-dead sister. Experimenting further, Hope discovered that he could routinely produce such effects, and he set about building a reputation as a spirit photographer. Skeptics insisted that Hope was a fraud, but their investigations never proved anything conclusive.*

8 MARCH

Mother Earth Day. *Almost all early cultures worshiped the earth as a mother goddess. In China, despite millennia of highly sophisticated civilization, this ancient notion has never completely vanished—even if it survives now only as tradition. Since long before environmental activists in the West ever heard of a green movement, the Chinese have been celebrating March 8 as Mother Earth's birthday.*

9 MARCH

Tibetan Butter Lamp Festival. *See above.*

10 MARCH

A noisy finish. *For the Ibo people of southern Nigeria, the traditional year expires at around this time on the modern calendar. As the moment approaches, villages erupt in a cacophony of noise, and children dash into their homes, fearful of being spirited away by the old year. Then the racket suddenly abates, and everyone reappears to welcome the new year with applause.*

From the Flames, A Prophecy of Revenge

One of the most remarkable institutions of the medieval era effectively came to an end on March 11, 1314, when King Philip IV of France had the last grand master of the Order of the Knights Templars, Jacques de Molay *(right)*, burned at the stake. As the flames licked at his flesh, de Molay predicted that Philip himself would be brought to eternal judgment within a year and that Pope Clement V, who had permitted the persecution of the Templars, would die within forty days. Both prophecies came true.

With this, the Order passed into legend. There were rumors that Templars survived as a secret sect for centuries thereafter, leaving their story mysteriously unfinished.

The Knights Templars (a name derived from the Temple of Solomon in Jerusalem, site of their first quarters) were founded in 1118 to protect Christian pilgrims visiting the Holy Land. They were superb warriors, giving no quarter in their battles with Muslims who were vying for the Holy Land. But in peace, they had much in common with other religious orders: The knights took vows of chastity and poverty and lived in dormitories.

Over the years, despite its members' vows of poverty, the Order grew prodigiously wealthy from gifts and the tax-exempt income of its estates. The Templars loaned money to many European monarchs, including Philip IV—and in the process, they stirred royal greed. The kingly debtors decided to simply seize the Templar wealth on the pretext that the Order had become corrupt, allegedly given to sexual perversion and devil worship. Evidence was manufactured by torture. Even de Molay confessed, but he then recanted. For this embarrassing hitch in his schemes, Philip had him burned alive, little dreaming that the grand master's death would soon be followed by his own.

11 MARCH

A fiery end for the Knights Templars. *See above.*

12 MARCH

The onion fields. *In times gone by, farmers of every land linked liturgical and agricultural timetables. Among English farmers of old, for example, this date—the feast day of Saint Gregory the Great, a pope who died in 604—was the deadline for the planting of onions.*

13 MARCH

A fortune fulfilled. *Seeking a glimpse of his future, an Elizabethan man-of-affairs named Henry Cuffe drew three Tarot cards. One depicted a man taken prisoner; the second was a scene of judgment; and the third showed a gallows. On March 13, 1601, Cuffe was hanged for plotting against Queen Elizabeth.*

14 MARCH

The Ghanaian New Year. *Instead of making a quick transition from the old year to the new, the people of Ghana spread their celebrations over thirteen days, the last one falling on the day after the spring equinox. The first eleven days are devoted to a series of dances performed for various purposes. Some are intended to drive away evil, others to honor the spirits of the dead, still others to bring good luck or to ensure a rich harvest. On the twelfth day, the spirits' shrines are washed clean of the old year and of any bad memories, while the thirteenth day is devoted to greeting the new year.*

A Memorable Medium

Eileen Garrett, a world-famous psychic credited with gifts of clairvoyance, telepathy, and precognition, was born on this day in 1893 in Ireland. During her fifty-year career, her purported psychic gifts were chiefly applied to making contact with the dead, most often through an Oriental spirit-guide who identified himself as Uvani. A woman of great liveliness and curiosity, Garrett studied exotic religions, funded expeditions to study unexplained phenomena, and established a research institute focusing on parapsychology. Scrupulously honest, she accepted no money for séances and even confessed to doubt the reality of her mediumistic powers, speculating that they were simply expressions of her subconscious. Yet in one carefully monitored test in New York, she identified items that were lying on a physician's desk in Iceland and even recited passages from a book the Icelandic doctor was reading at that moment.

The charred skeleton of British dirigible R101 clutters a hillside north of Paris in 1930; the crash took the lives of forty-six people. Months before the disaster, Irish-born medium Eileen Garrett (left) allegedly experienced premonitory visions of a blimp falling out of the sky, and the spirits of dead aviators had frequented her séances with warnings of an impending tragedy.

15 MARCH

"Beware the Ides of March." Shakespeare did not invent the supernatural warnings of Julius Caesar's assassination on this day in 44 BC. Second-century biographer Plutarch wrote that a soothsayer warned Caesar "to take heed" on March 15, "for on that day he should be in grave danger." Plutarch also recorded that Caesar's wife Calpurnia begged him not to go out because she had dreamed he would be slain. Caesar went anyway. Near the Senate he saw the soothsayer and "merrily" noted, "The Ides of March be come." Yes, agreed the prophet softly, "but yet are they not past." Just moments later Caesar's colleagues slashed him to death.

16 MARCH

A festival of color. Over several days preceding the full moon of March, the Hindu festival of Holi celebrates the arrival of spring and commemorates the downfall of the legendary demon Holika, who was burned to death for devouring children. A distinctive feature of Holi is the playful throwing or smearing (below) of abir, a crimson powder.

17 MARCH

Birthday of an amazing woman. See above.

18 MARCH

Renowned psychic. Famed clairvoyant and psychic healer Edgar Cayce, who during trances often described life in the lost land of Atlantis, was born March 18, 1877.

Sheelah's Day. In Ireland, this date was once set aside to honor Sheelahna-gig, the goddess of fertility, represented below in the stonework of a church. When Christianity came to Ireland, the pagan deity took on a new identity as a relative of Saint Patrick—in some accounts his wife, in others his mother.

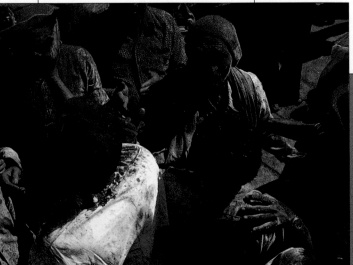

Aries: March 21-April 20

To the ancients, the sun appeared to make a slow annual orbit around a stationary earth, and stargazers divided the circle described by the sun's progress into twelve constellations—the signs of the zodiac. On March 21, the first flickers of spring rouse the northern reaches of the planet from their winter slumber, and thus astrologers denoted Aries, the sector the sun enters on that date, as the first sign of the zodiac.

Those born when the sun is in Aries are said to be willful, like their feisty animal totem, the Ram. They are also considered aggressive, influenced by Mars—the planet named for the Roman warrior god. Furthermore, Aries is thought to govern the head, which imparts an oft-foolhardy impulsiveness upon those born under the sign.

Lacking foresight, they frequently charge headlong into any interest that grabs their fancy, oblivious to the consequences for themselves or others. Like the element fire, with which their sign is associated, they

have the potential to destroy whatever lies in their path.

Natives of Aries answer to no one. They enjoy wielding power themselves, however, and can be domineering in personal relationships. Driven by fierce independence, they tend to be wary of emotional commitment and have a penchant for short-lived romances.

Their best quality is said to be courage. Known to dare under circumstances others dread, Arians are the world's adventurers and history's pioneers. Some famous Arians include Sandra Day O'Connor, first woman on the U.S. Supreme Court; magician Harry Houdini; painter Vincent van Gogh; and Gloria Steinem, writer and feminist leader.

19 MARCH

An annual miracle. *As if watching a calendar, migrating swallows return from their winter homes to a summering place near California's old mission town of San Juan Capistrano on this same date every year, Saint Joseph's Day.*

The Babylonian New Year. *Akitu, Babylonia's ten-day-long New Year festival, was held around the time of the spring equinox and was a celebration of the marriage of heaven and earth.*

20 MARCH

Festival of Isis. *In ancient Egypt, the spring harvest festival, held to honor the goddess Isis (below), began on this date. Isis was a deity-of-all-trades, worshiped not only as mother goddess and enchantress but also as protector of the dead and patroness of seafarers.*

21 MARCH

The sun enters the sign of Aries. *See above.*

22 MARCH

A witches' celebration. *The modern branch of witchcraft known as Wicca observes a joyous holiday on the vernal equinox, which falls generally either on this date or a day or two earlier. The witches call the feast Eostre, after the Teutonic goddess of spring, and mark it with rituals of renewal and rebirth. Eggs are the primary symbol of Eostre; dyed and decorated, they are as much a part of some Wiccan rituals as of the Christian Easter.*

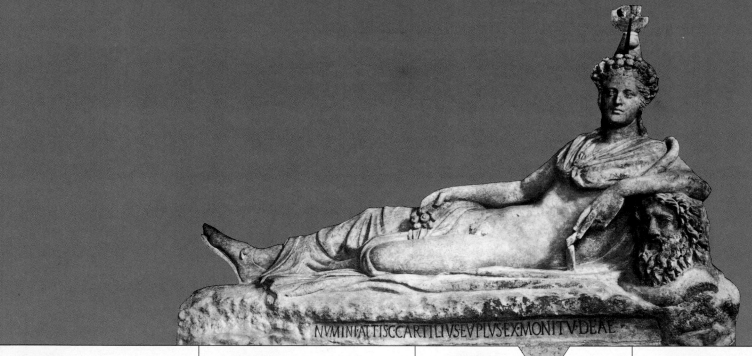

23 MARCH

Away with winter. *As spring nears, old people in the Polish countryside prepare to send winter packing with the festival of Marzenna. They weave straw dolls that represent the waning season, each three or four feet tall, dressed in rags and festooned with ribbons (below). When mild weather tells the villagers spring has arrived, they sing and dance as they carry the straw figures to nearby rivers or lakes and toss them into the icy waters.*

24 MARCH

Passover. *Originally a spring harvest festival, Passover is today an eight-day celebration of the "passing-over" of the houses of the Jews by an angel that God sent to slay the firstborn sons of Egypt. A moveable feast, it begins at the full moon nearest the spring equinox. Its centerpiece is a ritual family meal known as the seder, during which prayers are recited and the story of the Exodus is read. The meal is rich in symbolic details and touches of drama: At one point, for example, the door of the house is opened, and the prophet Elijah is invited to enter in and drink from a goblet of wine.*

25 MARCH

Divine renewal. *In late March, Romans honored a pair of ill-fated lovers, the mother goddess Cybele and a young shepherd named Attis (above). According to myth, Attis castrated himself in a moment of madness and bled to death. Cybele begged Jupiter to restore his life, and the supreme deity responded by transforming the body into a pine tree, eternally green. The cult of Cybele was served in Rome by self-castrated priests. Toward the end of the March rites, they carried a pine to her temple, then slashed themselves and splattered the altar with blood. On March 25, this mourning gave way to an ecstatic debauch of eating and drinking.*

26 MARCH

A time of gestation. *By old Slavic mystical tradition, March 26 was designated as the start of the plowing season, because the earth was thought to be pregnant until this day. It would be a sin to till the soil of the expectant mother with any kind of iron implement.*

An Elaborate Balancing Act

Once in a century—but more often if times are particularly troublesome—the people of Bali gather to restore the balance between the forces of good and evil. This harmonizing feat, accomplished by means of a festival called Eka Dasa Rudra, is not a simple one. Eka Dasa Rudra lasts eleven weeks and consists of some thirty ceremonies, ranging from sacred dances to a three-day, thirty-eight-mile-long procession *(right)* from a temple complex atop Mount Agung—Bali's holiest volcano—to the sea and back again.

The climax of the festival occurs on March 28, when tens of thousands of pilgrims crowd the temple complex and watch as scores of animals are sacrificed in an effort to slake the fury of Rudra, the evil side of Bali's supreme deity. After that ancient rite has been carried out, dancers perform elaborate figures, gifts are offered up to the gods, and priests direct prayers in all eleven directions of Balinese space. Thus the festival is brought to a close until another hundred years have gone by—or until some sudden tilt of the scales in favor of the forces of malevolence prompts remedial action.

27 MARCH

Passage into adulthood. *For Roman males, the festival of Liberalia, held on March 27 in honor of the vegetation god Liber, marked the transition from boyhood to manhood. Boys who had reached a suitable age—usually seventeen—doffed their purple-bordered togas, put on the plain togas worn by men, and assumed the status of citizens.*

28 MARCH

A visionary saint. *The Spanish mystic known as Saint Teresa of Ávila entered the world on March 28, 1515, and, in effect, left it some twenty years later when she joined the austere order of Carmelite nuns. Over the years, she committed her mystical beliefs to paper, writing with great power and passion. In a book titled The Interior Castle, she laid out the path that a soul must follow in order to achieve union with God. She also left vivid descriptions of her visions, voices she heard, and "raptures" that lifted her bodily off the ground.*

29 MARCH

A yearly correction. *Believing that the equilibrium of sun, rain, and soil is upset by farming, the Bobo people of Africa perform a restorative masquerade each year on this date. Clad in special costumes and wearing painted masks (below), they beg an intermediary god to redress the natural balance, banish evil, and bring the rainfall that will ensure a good harvest.*

30 MARCH

The trembling earth. *Iran's New Year celebration begins at the spring equinox and lasts for thirteen days. Families light small bonfires and jump over them, symbolically leaping into the new year. As with so many spring ceremonies, eggs play a part—in this case symbolizing an ancient belief that the earth trembles at the arrival of a new year. As the moment of transition nears, an egg is placed upon a mirror, and almost always shivers slightly—if only because of excitement in the room.*

31 MARCH

The Fox sisters' debut. *In upstate New York on the last day of March 1848, two sisters, Kate and Maggie Fox (below), touched off a craze for spiritualism when, for the first time, they apparently communicated with the dead, who tapped out responses to their questions. Forty years later, the sisters admitted to faking the episode. By then, however, spiritualists practicing their techniques numbered in the tens of thousands.*

1 APRIL

A day for pranks. *Mystery surrounds the origin of April Fool's Day, an occasion for playing pranks and making fun of others. The spirit of the day has been linked to the uncertain weather at that time of year, to an old custom of letting the insane out of asylums one day each year for the amusement of normal folk, and even to the story of Christ's passion, during which Jesus was shunted pointlessly from place to place, only to be mocked and tormented.*

2 APRIL

The demise of winter. *The fourth Sunday in Lent, named Rejoicing Day after a biblical verse from the Book of Isaiah, long retained a pagan flavor among German people. In some places, a fight was staged by two men, one dressed as winter and the other attired as spring, with the latter always emerging the victor. Elsewhere, people would create straw dolls, then burn or drown them—a ceremony they called "carrying death away."*

3 APRIL

The thirteenth day. *Iranians observe a holiday called Sizdar-Bedah on the thirteenth day of their New Year, or No Ruz, festival. It is considered unlucky to stay indoors on this day, so people flock to their favorite picnic spots. On the way, children throw bowls of sprouted seeds into streams in the belief that the old year's bad luck will be swept away with this offering.*

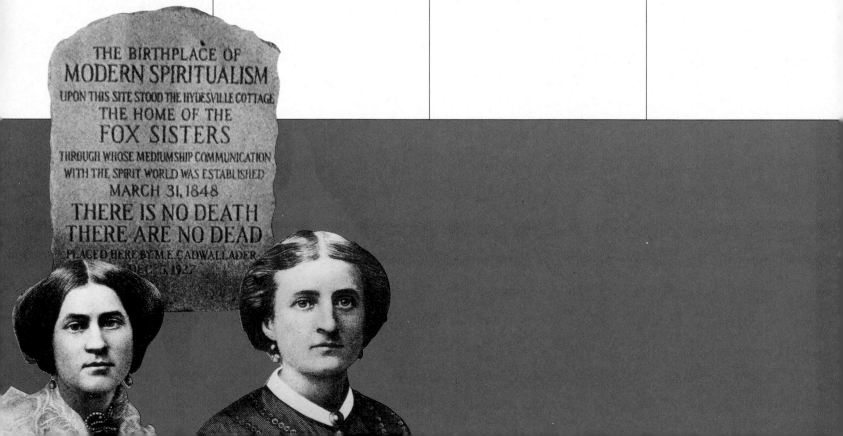

THE BIRTHPLACE OF
MODERN SPIRITUALISM
UPON THIS SITE STOOD THE HYDESVILLE COTTAGE
THE HOME OF THE
FOX SISTERS
THROUGH WHOSE MEDIUMSHIP COMMUNICATION
WITH THE SPIRIT WORLD WAS ESTABLISHED
MARCH 31, 1848
THERE IS NO DEATH
THERE ARE NO DEAD
PLACED HERE BY M. E. CADWALLADER
DEC. 5, 1927

When the Pharaoh's Curse Struck Home

In 1922, after fifteen years of labor in Egypt's Valley of the Kings, excavators in the employ of archaeologist Howard Carter and his sponsor, George Edward Herbert, fifth earl of Carnarvon, made a sensational discovery. They broke through into an underground tomb that held a rich collection of jewelry, chariots, thrones, and other artifacts to serve the occupant in the afterlife. Continued digging revealed an even more extraordinary treasure: The tomb also contained the mummy of a boy-king who had died thirty centuries earlier. The pharaoh Tutankhamen, or Tut as he came to be known by the press,

lay sealed in a chamber just a few meters away. Lord Carnarvon, however, would not live long enough to see the mummy disinterred. He was bitten by a mosquito when he went to visit the newly opened tomb, and on April 5, about five months after the initial discovery, he joined King Tut in death, succumbing to a mysterious blood infection.

Some attributed his demise to a "Pharaoh's curse"—vengeance for defilement of the royal resting place. It was said that at the precise moment he died, the lights of Cairo flickered and, far away in England, the earl's dog howled, then expired as well.

4 APRIL

Homage to Cybele. *Threatened by the armies of Hannibal in 205 BC, the leaders of Rome delved into a canon of prophecies known as the Sibylline Books. In this oracular source, they found a prediction saying that Hannibal would be driven from Italy, and within a year the prophecy was fulfilled. Ever ready to add a new festival to the calendar, the Romans set aside April 4 as a day on which to honor their protector, Cybele.*

5 APRIL

An alien issue for Congress. *On this date in 1966, responding to a flurry of UFO sightings, the House Committee on Armed Services commenced a brief and—for the most part—closed-door hearing on the issue of possible alien visitations. Only a handful of witnesses were called to give testimony, and their opinions were generally supportive of the longstanding government view that UFO sightings have natural explanations. Ufologists were less than convinced that the proceedings were thorough.*

6 APRIL

A spring festival for children. *On this day in southeastern France, children cast miniature pine boats into the estuaries of the Moselle River in an annual celebration of spring. Each boat has a lighted candle in place of a mast, symbolizing humankind's joy in sailing the seas of life.*

7 APRIL

Secret benefactors. *In Rumania, offerings are made on this day to the spirits of the water and the underworld. Though hidden, they apparently are deemed beneficent if given their proper due: They go by the name of Blajini, or "kindly ones."*

Folk Beliefs of Holy Week

Usually in April but sometimes in March, depending on the phase of the moon, the season of Lent draws to a close with Holy Week, a series of religious observances commemorating the passion and death of Jesus Christ. Over the centuries, numerous folk beliefs have attached themselves to the week's Christian framework. For example, on Palm Sunday—a day celebrating the joyous reception of Jesus in Jerusalem by a palm-waving crowd—churchgoers in some parts of Greece receive branches of evergreen myrtle or bay along with the usual crosses of woven palm leaves; mothers use these leafy bunches to protect their children against the evil eye.

Good Friday, the day of the Crucifixion, has attracted an abundance of traditions. According to one belief, planting a garden on Good Friday guarantees profusion. Similarly, a friend acquired on that day is supposedly a friend for life. Evil can be averted by baking hot cross buns on Good Friday and then hanging them over the bed.

Many of the traditions linked to Holy Week have clear pagan ancestry. Hot cross buns, for instance, can be traced to the cross-inscribed loaves that Romans baked in honor of Diana, goddess of the hunt. And the origin of a longstanding taboo against fishing on Good Friday can be found in the cult once associated with Atargatis, an ancient goddess whose day was Friday and to whom fish were sacred.

Wearing halos, silver robes, and feathery wings, girls lead a procession through the town of Ouro Prêto, in southeastern Brazil, to mark the end of Holy Week.

8 APRIL

Bottling up winter. *When their corn has been planted, the Cuchumatan Indians of Guatemala take pains to protect against winter's return. Villagers climb to a nearby cliff where Frost is said to live. A shaman is lowered by rope to a crack in the cliff's face, which he plasters shut to seal in the killing cold.*

Listening to the universe. *This date in 1960 saw the start of Project Ozma, a pioneering attempt by astronomer Frank Drake and his colleagues at the National Radio Astronomy Observatory in West Virginia to detect messages from alien civilizations with a radio telescope.*

9 APRIL

Feast of A-Ma. *In the tiny Portuguese territory of Macao, situated on a peninsula along China's southern coast, this day is devoted to praises of the goddess A-Ma, patroness of sailors and fishermen. Macao's very name honors her: It is derived from the Chinese word A-mangao, "bay of the goddess A-Ma."*

10 APRIL

A mysterious sea monster. *On April 10, 1977, a Japanese trawler hauled in a carcass (below) that some investigators took to be the remains of a plesiosaur, a huge and supposedly extinct reptile (below, right) that paddled the world's oceans 100 million years ago. Skeptics contend that the catch was most likely a basking shark.*

11 APRIL

Holy Week. *See above.*

A Preview of Disaster?

Was the sinking of the *Titanic* foreseen fourteen years before it happened? If so, the 2,224 people aboard the great ocean liner on its maiden voyage in April of 1912 certainly were unaware of it. They believed they were on the world's safest ship. The huge floating palace was thought so sturdy that the owners considered sinking to be an impossibility. They equipped the vessel with only twenty lifeboats, which could carry fewer than 1,200 people. As a result, when the *Titanic* collided with an iceberg on April 14 and suffered a fatal tear in its hull, 1,513 people perished. The famed liner would not be seen again until a deep-sea camera discovered its grave in 1985 *(above)*.

But in a sense, the *Titanic* was following a script—a novel, extraordinarily prescient in its details, that was published fourteen years earlier by an American writer named Morgan Robertson. For his tale, Robertson invented a British liner, the S.S. *Titan,* describing it as the biggest and safest vessel in the world. The size, speed, and passenger capacity he gave to the *Titan* were almost exactly those of the *Titanic.* Like the *Titanic,* the fictional *Titan* first put to sea in April, struck an iceberg on its starboard side, and sank with a huge loss of life.

At the very least, the similarity of the two ships and their fates was extraordinarily coincidental, but some people have seen it as more than that: The author, they note, considered himself something of a psychic and once claimed that he owed his inspiration to what he called his "astral writing partner." But Robertson shed no light on the issue. He died, destitute and forgotten, three years after the *Titanic* went to the bottom.

12 APRIL

A resourceful lover. *The Nepalese New Year falls in the middle of an eight-day April festival called Bisket, linked to an ancient account of a princess possessed by two serpent demons. The princess took many lovers, it is said, and all died in her bed. Then a prince of a foreign land arrived and arranged a tryst. That night, after lovemaking, he hid himself and watched the princess for hours. Finally, two threads of darkness emerged from her nostrils and expanded into serpents. Leaping from concealment, the prince slew the demons with his sword, then devoted himself to the pleasures of love once again.*

13 APRIL

A festival of water. *For three days in April, Buddhists in Thailand welcome the new year with a ceremony of cleansing. During the celebrations, statues of the Buddha are ritually bathed, and people throw water at one another to wash away the old year's evil.*

14 APRIL

The sinking of the Titanic. *See above.*

15 APRIL

Sacrificing the unborn. *In the Roman calendar, this day was set aside for an offering to Tellus, the earth mother. To ensure that their farms would be productive, people sacrificed a pregnant cow and burned the unborn calf.*

Pre-Christian Links to the Holiest Christian Day

The resurrection of Jesus Christ is celebrated on Easter, the culmination of Holy Week and the most important festival of the Christian calendar. It is a moveable feast, occurring on the first Sunday after the first full moon after the spring equinox—a formula devised at the Council of Nicea, a gathering of bishops held in the year 325. Consequently, Easter can fall on any Sunday between March 22 and April 25. (The Orthodox Church observes Easter a week later, on the second Sunday after the first full moon of spring.)

During the early days of Christianity, Easter was linked to the festival of Passover. The Council of Nicea severed that tie, but the influence of many other non-Christian religious traditions can still be discerned. Eggs, for example, were a symbol of fertility in many pagan cultures. Church leaders forbade the eating of them during Lent but lifted the prohibition on Easter. The practice of dyeing and decorating eggs probably originated in Middle Eastern spring festivals and spread to Europe during the time of the Crusades.

The tradition of an Easter Bunny is Teutonic in origin: A hare—a prolific breeder that came to be associated with the laying of Easter eggs—was the emblem of Eostre, the Teutonic goddess of spring, who gave Easter its name. Even the custom of wearing new clothes on Easter can be traced to pagan times, when people chose the time of spring festivals to shed the old and don the new.

16 APRIL

Easter. *See above.*

17 APRIL

A patriot's wish. *On this day in 1790, American statesman Benjamin Franklin died, having harbored for many years an interest in the possibility of bringing the dead back to life. On one occasion, he noticed that flies that he had presumed drowned in a bottle of wine revived when he placed them in the sun, and he hypothesized that humans might also be retrieved from death. Indeed, he jestingly wrote to a friend that because of his "ardent desire to see the state of America a hundred years hence," he would "prefer to an ordinary death being immersed with a few friends in a cask of Madeira," from which he could be "recalled to life."*

18 APRIL

Rama's Day. *A paragon of chivalry and virtue, the Hindu god Rama was the seventh of the ten incarnations of the god Vishnu and the husband of the goddess Sita. The festival of Ram Navami, staged at this time of year, commemorates Rama's royal birth as the first son of King Dasaratha. As part of the festivities, Hindus retell their favorite stories from the epic poem, the Ramayana, or "romance of Rama."*

19 APRIL

Death of Lord Byron. *Many foreign romantics have fallen in love with Greece, but English poet George Gordon, Lord Byron, may be the only one who truly left his heart there. Idolized for work such as Childe Harold's Pilgrimage, Byron also had an interest in the occult. He helped shape Mary Shelley's Frankenstein, and he gave John Polidori the idea for The Vampyre, a novel that led to all the vampire books, plays, and movies since. Byron died of a fever on this day in 1824 while helping Greeks fight for independence from the Ottomans. His corpse was shipped to England, except for his heart, which was buried in Greece.*

Taurus: April 21–May 20

As the early, unpredictable days of spring soften into the more settled weather of late April and May, so too does volatile Aries give way to steady Taurus. Astrologers say that unlike reckless Aries, Taurus is all level-headed maturity: practical, patient, and, like its symbol—the Bull—a bastion of strength and a bulwark against adversity.

It is said that those born under the sign of Taurus stubbornly pursue any goal. They are loyal friends and tender lovers, tolerant of the foibles of others and slow to anger. Once roused, however, their fury is frightful, making the choice of the Bull as the Taurean symbol all the more appropriate.

Taurus is also identified with the element earth, a connection that fuels its natives' worldly approach to life. Tireless at work and passionate at play, Taureans meet life's challenges head-on and revel in its pleasures. Indeed, they are the world's most ardent materialists and its most blatant sensualists, guided by Venus, planet of the Roman goddess of love. They display an uncanny knack for earning money, which they use to feather their own nests.

Allowed to run unchecked, Taurean materialism may teeter into greed, and bullish determination can become bullheaded obstinacy. In addition, the combination of devotion and desire that often makes a Taurean the ideal spouse can explode into fiery jealousy.

On balance, however, Taureans are the stalwarts of the zodiac, and their ranks include military great Ulysses S. Grant—typically Taurean in his dogged pursuit of victory in the American Civil War—British Queen Elizabeth II, tennis player Chris Evert, and actress Shirley MacLaine.

20 APRIL

A craving for power. *In 1889, Adolf Hitler (below) was born on this date in the village of Braunau in Austria. Destined to show malignant genius at building political and military power, he was also intrigued by the hidden powers of the mind. On one occasion during World War I, he left his trench position just moments before an artillery round struck—a narrow escape that he attributed to clairvoyance.*

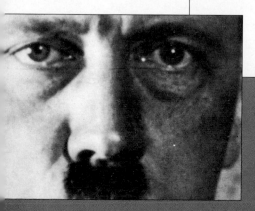

21 APRIL

Guardians of livestock. *Each year on this date, the Romans honored a pair of deities known as the Pales, the guardians of cattle and sheep. Ritual cleaning of the stalls, offerings to the gods, and the purification of the animals were all part of the day's activities, which ended with a feast after the herdsmen had leaped three times over a bonfire. Eventually, the festival became one of the most important on the Roman calendar: April 21, it was decided, was the day on which Romulus had founded the city of Rome.*

22 APRIL

A ghostly train. *The grief that followed the assassination of President Abraham Lincoln in 1865 had no precedent in American history. Seven million people—a quarter of the nation's population—paid their respects as the dead president was slowly carried home to Illinois by a funeral train. Some say the train repeats the mournful journey every April, making a spectral transit along a stretch of track in New York State. A military band is supposedly aboard, playing music beyond the range of mortal ears.*

23 APRIL

A leader from another time. *Both brave and pious in rare measure, the legendary Christian warrior known as Saint George lived in Asia Minor in the third century AD. He reputedly slew a dragon and performed other knightly deeds, then died a martyr's death on April 23, 303. After the Crusades, he became England's patron saint, and as late as World War I, British soldiers reported seeing him riding into battle.*

Dark Night and Shining Day

In German tradition, the hours of darkness after sunset on April 30 and before sunrise on May 1 are known as Walpurgis Night, named for Saint Walpurga, an abbess who died in AD 779. Despite the saintly provenance, *Walpurgisnacht* belongs to witches. Legend says that on this blackest of nights, they fly in from every corner, clutching broomsticks and spewing evil, to gather atop the Brocken—the highest peak in the Harz Mountains. There, they share a night of feasting and licentious revelry with the devil.

In times past, people sought to frighten off the witches by making as much noise as they could during the night, ringing church bells, slamming doors, cracking whips, and banging pots and pans. They lit bonfires, erected crosses, and brandished torches topped with such supposed witch-dispersants as rosemary and juniper, and they witch-proofed their houses by decking the doors and windows with birch boughs. Not until dawn dispelled the darkness could people at last let down their guard.

These customs have faded, but Walpurgis Night retains great importance for modern witches, followers of the Wiccan faith. This date ranks among their most sacred sabbats, or festivals, and is a hallowed prelude to their annual celebration of Beltane on the first day of May.

Beltane—or May Day, as it is known nowadays to non-witches—stands in bright contrast to dark Walpurgis Night. In Celtic tradition, the beginning of May marked the start of summer. Huge bonfires were lit on the hilltops, sometimes near a sacred tree representing the gods of vegetation—a practice that gave rise to the tradition of the maypole. Once the bonfires were blazing, the people danced around them, singing and moving in a clockwise direction. Sometimes bonfires were kindled in pairs, and the merrymakers danced and drove their cattle between them as a rite of purification.

Beltane was suppressed by the Catholic church, but pagan practices long continued to greet the month of May. In England and elsewhere, young men and maidens would go a-Maying on the eve of May Day, spending the night in the greenwood and returning at dawn to dress the village in boughs of greenery and garlands of flowers—a custom that came to be called "bringing in the May." On their way home, the young women, some no longer maidens, might pause to wash their faces in the morning dew, which was said to have the power to preserve or restore one's looks.

The returning Maying parties might also carry home a birch or pine tree stripped of all its branches. Placed upright on the village green and gaily decorated with vines, flowers, and ribbons, it became the maypole—an obvious phallic symbol, linked to the fertility of crops, cattle, and people.

In times past, nearly every village had its own maypole; in fact, London had several, including a 134-foot-tall giant that was erected in 1661 and that held its ground for more than fifty years. In many places, a May King and Queen would also be chosen, and under their aegis people would dance around the maypole from morning to night on the first day of May.

Maypoles fell into disfavor during the heyday of Puritanism in the mid-seventeenth century, with one noteworthy defender of public morality indicting the maypole as a "stinckying idoll." In time, what had been a carefree fertility festival was stripped of its religious and magical significance and became little more than an official holiday—in some places chosen, with no evident awareness of the irony, for displays of military power. Nowadays the old Beltane customs are mainly observed only by witches.

24 APRIL

A window on the future. *In rural areas of England, it was once a practice for those who sought a glimpse of the future to spend this night—Saint Mark's Eve—on the porch of the local church. Sometime during the night, the spirits of all those destined to die in the next year would supposedly glide by. The preview had its price, however, since those who stood watch had to remain awake—or never wake again. Moreover, they had to repeat the vigil each year thereafter for the rest of their lives.*

25 APRIL

A fungal god. *In order to protect their life-giving crops, the ancient Romans went to a grove outside the city each year on this day and sacrificed a dog and a sheep to Robigus, the god of mildew.*

26 APRIL

A propitiating start. *In the African republic of Sierra Leone, this day—the start of their new year—is devoted to a seed-sowing ceremony (below) that is designed to appease the goddess of fertility.*

27 APRIL

Homage to Tyi Wara. *Farmers of the Bambara tribe in Mali attribute their food-growing ability to a mythical teacher named Tyi Wara, half-man, half-animal (below). On this day, they honor his memory with songs and dance.*

Gaily costumed, modern pagans weave colored ribbons around a maypole in a symbolic fertility dance said to meld male and female energy.

28 APRIL

A celebration of sex. *In imperial Rome, six days of government-sanctioned debauchery got underway on April 28. The festival of Floralia—honoring Flora, goddess of flowering plants—began with a play that featured nude actresses and obscene gestures and dances. Ribald games followed, including the snaring of such notably libidinous animals as hares and goats. In later years, young men took to expressing their ardor by erecting trees or poles in front of the houses of favored women—a precursor of the maypoles that became a part of May Day celebrations in Europe.*

29 APRIL

The prophet's ascension. *According to Islamic tradition, the prophet Muhammad had a vision in which he flew astride a mythical beast called the Buraq from Mecca to Jerusalem in a single night. From there, he ascended to the heavenly throne of God, where he was told to recite a prayer called the salat fifty times a day. That number was later reduced to five, and today all Muslims pray the salat five times daily. Muhammad's vision is recalled by the faithful on this date with readings of the account of the journey.*

30 APRIL

Walpurgis Night. *See above.*

1 MAY

Reading forbidden books. *On this date in 1776, Bavarian lawyer Adam Weishaupt (below, left) founded the Order of the Illuminati, a secret society dedicated to the study of books banned by the Jesuit religious order. Assuming the name Spartacus, Weishaupt established three degrees of membership: Novice, Minerval, and Illuminated Minerval. Promotion was marked by ceremonies involving disclosure of secret signs and passwords. Though never large, the society included such notables as the dukes of Brunswick and Gotha. Disbanded in 1795, the Illuminati reappeared in 1906 and again in the 1980s.*

2 MAY

Magical horses. *A European reminder of May Day's origins as a fertility festival is the hobbyhorse—a man dressed in equine costume, often wearing a pointed hat and a fiendish mask. One such apparition romps through the English town of Minehead (above) from May Day eve through May 2. Until recently, the hobbyhorse was attended by two club-wielding assistants whose job was to prompt donations from the crowd.*

3 MAY

D-Day puzzle. *British agents were concerned on May 3, 1944, when the secret code word Utah—designating a landing beach for the coming invasion of France—appeared in the London Daily Telegraph crossword puzzle solution. Concern became alarm as numerous code words appeared in subsequent puzzles—including, only days before the invasion, Overlord, the operation's code name. Suspecting espionage, agents swarmed into the paper's office to confront the puzzle setter. Questioning revealed he was no spy, but he could not account for the amazing coincidence. Some wonder if he picked up unintended psychic messages, or perhaps foresaw the future.*

4 MAY

Frustrating the fairies. *The Irish once believed that fairies emerged from hiding at this time of year to make trouble for humans. People limited their travel to avoid running afoul of the sprites, and some wore their coats inside out to confuse the fairies. A spot of tea and a bit of bread left on the doorstep were thought to deter trickery, but babies were always guarded lest the wee folk kidnap them and leave ugly changelings in their stead. Today, some believers in UFOs speculate that abductions by aliens led to the tales of fairies kidnapping children.*

5 MAY

Rain festival. *In parts of Mexico and Central America, some such as the Yucatán priest above still offer prayers to a rain god. Guatemalans of the old faith mark May 5 with a rain goddess ritual.*

The reappearance of Mu. *The fabled lost Pacific continent called Mu will rise from its watery grave on this date in the year 2000, according to the Lemurian Fellowship. This group says Mu once stretched from North America to Asia and was home to the utopian Mukulian Empire before sinking into the sea.*

Dance from the Distant Past

Although it coincides with the feast of Saint Michael the Archangel on May 8, the so-called Furry Dance held in the Cornish town of Helston, on England's southwestern tip, predates the Christian era. The dance is, in fact, one of the world's oldest surviving spring festivals. The name Furry may come from Flora, the Roman goddess of flowers, or perhaps is an echo of the Celtic word for "fair." Whatever its etymological lineage, the festival preserves the essence of countless spring-welcoming ceremonies in the dim past: It brings people together for communal dancing, a demonstration of their unity.

The ceremonies consist chiefly of a day-long series of processions, first by young men and women, then by children, and finally by the more prominent citizens of the area. Assembled in long lines and led by a band, they weave in and out of houses and gardens, along the town streets, and through public buildings. Wherever the celebrants wander, it is said, good fortune will follow.

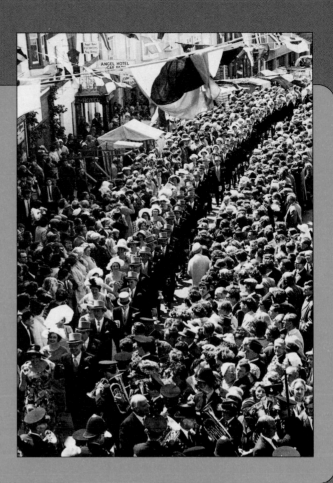

6 MAY

Noah's Ark runs aground. *According to James Ussher, a seventeenth-century bishop of Armagh and primate of Ireland, Noah's Ark settled on the mountains of Ararat on May 6, 2349 BC, a precise date he determined by consulting "sacred and exotic history, astronomical calculation" and an old "Hebrew calendar." Furthermore, declared the prelate, the day of the week was Wednesday.*

7 MAY

English Hocktide. *On the third Monday and Tuesday after Easter, villagers traditionally used ropes to "hock," or catch, a member of the opposite sex. The captive gained release by donating to the local church.*

8 MAY

A dream of devastation. *In the spring of 1902, a British soldier who was to become an aviation pioneer, John William Dunne, dreamed about an island doomed by a volcano. In the dream, Dunne said, he tried in vain to persuade "incredulous French authorities" to evacuate the island. Not long after, he read in a newspaper that on May 8, Mount Pelée on the French West Indian island of Martinique had erupted with horrific violence, killing some 30,000 people. More predictive dreams in later years prompted Dunne to develop a new theory of time to account for his premonitions.*

9 MAY

Days of dread. *Ancient Romans believed that on May 9, 11, and 13, the gate between this world and the next opened, allowing restless spirits, or lemures, to pour through. Pacifying the ghosts required the male head of every household to arise at midnight on each of the three nights, wash his hands three times, then stride through the house spitting or tossing black beans behind him for the ghosts to gather. This sequence was repeated nine times. Finally, he would wash his hands again, strike a brass vessel, and call out nine times, "Shades of my fathers, depart." Despite these measures, the lemures cast a pall over the month, giving rise to the belief that May marriages are unwise.*

England's Medieval Capers

In some parts of England, no spring festival would be complete without an appearance by the local band of Morris dancers. Although the origin of their name is obscure—some believe it was another term for pagan—a medieval inheritance is clear.

Dressed in white and wearing brightly colored sashes, their straw hats strung with ribbons and hung with flowers, the dancers step and stomp to the measure of fiddles and accordions. Jingling bells strapped to their legs add to the hoopla. The dances, sometimes graceful, at other times charged with energy, are performed according to complex patterns and may be accompanied by clapping, waving of handkerchiefs, or rhythmic stamping of short staves on the ground.

Morris dancers make their first appearance of the year on May Day, perform again on the Whit holiday weekend (Whitsunday is the seventh Sunday after Easter) and reappear occasionally throughout the summer. By tradition, they are always men, generally organized into troupes consisting of six dancers, a musician, and a fool, who may poke at women with a horse effigy fixed to the front of his waist and uses a bladder strung to a stick to keep the crowds at bay.

10 MAY

Happy anniversary. *On May 6, Madurai, India, celebrates the marriage of the god Shiva (below right) to goddess Meenakshi (center). Her brother Vishnu (left) gives her away.*

11 MAY

England's ubiquitous Morris dancers. *See above.*

12 MAY

No nine lives. *To prove cats are not magical, a tenth-century Flemish count tossed some from a high tower. His deed is recalled in Ypres by the Cat Parade (below).*

13 MAY

A holy vision. *On May 13, 1917, at Fátima, Portugal, the Virgin Mary allegedly made the first of six appearances to three peasant children, an event that was to rivet the world's attention (see October 13).*

Virgins and Straw Men

During the course of the year, Rome's vestal virgins—the six priestesses of the goddess Vesta—not only tended a sacred fire in their temple *(see March 1)* but also played a role in numerous religious festivals. One of the celebrations was the annual Argei rites held on May 15. The Argei, or, more properly, the *argeorum sacraria,* were twenty-seven shrines scattered around the city and said to have been consecrated by the early Roman king Numa (twenty-seven because it was three times nine, and therefore a magic number). On this day, the shrines became way stations for a solemn procession led by the vestal virgins, the Pontifex Maximus, or chief priest, and a few magistrates.

At each of the Argei, the paraders paused to pick up a straw puppet made to resemble an old man. Once all twenty-seven puppets had been collected, they were carried to the Pons Sublicius, Rome's oldest bridge, and thrown into the Tiber River by the virgins.

Exactly why the Romans created an elaborate ceremony around heaving straw dolls into a river remains uncertain. Possibly the rite was a purification ceremony preparatory to some larger agricultural ritual. Perhaps it was intended to propitiate a river god. Or, according to some scholars, the ritual may have recalled an earlier time when old men were tossed into the river as human sacrifices to the god Saturn.

The old wooden Sublicius bridge, from which straw men were thrown into the Tiber, stood near here. Before 100 BC it was replaced by the stone Ponte Rotto (foreground).

14 MAY

The midnight sun. *On May 14 in far northern Norway, the rising sun begins a ''day'' that will last ten weeks. Changes in both social and physiological activity occasioned by the midnight sun—people easily get by with little sleep, working and playing almost around the clock— demonstrate how strongly human behavior is tied to the earth's natural rhythms, even in a sophisticated civilization. Come November, when sunset plunges the region into two months of darkness, life slows and people sleep more.*

15 MAY

A heave-ho for straw men. *See above.*

16 MAY

Death of a medium. *This day in 1918 marked the death of famed Italian medium Eusapia Palladino. Her alleged ability to levitate objects— during one séance she reportedly lifted herself, bound in a chair, onto the top of a table—earned her the nickname Queen of the Cabinet, after the curtain-enclosed space in which mediums supposedly concentrate their psychic energy. Though Palladino was caught faking her stunts on a number of occasions, she performed many feats that left even the most ardent skeptics thoroughly perplexed.*

17 MAY

A modern fertility rite. *On this day in the town of Obando, in the Philippine islands, childless couples seek to improve their luck in starting families by dancing at a special fertility festival. The objective of the dance is to win the intercession of the Catholic saints.*

Gemini: May 21-June 21

Beginning on May 21, Gemini straddles the seasons of spring and summer, in the process betraying what astrologers describe as the duality inherent in the sign. Gemini's double personality is apparent in its zodiacal symbol, the Twins, and is said to be equally obvious in the behavior of its natives, whose hallmark is inconsistency.

Indeed, thanks to the influence of the planet Mercury, quicksilvery Geminis lead lives of fluctuation. They are consummate fence-sitters, able to see two points of view at the same time—and to argue both sides convincingly. Their ruling element is air, which contributes to their elusiveness.

Geminis are full of charm and wit, although their ready sense of humor often masks their true feelings. Unlike conservative Taureans, Gemini natives have little respect for tradition and constantly seek out change. Spontaneity is their stock in trade and monotony a curse, whether in their professions or in affairs of the heart. Consequently, Geminis fall in—and out—of love with ease and tend to shy away from long-term commitments.

On the job, Geminis are ill-suited to the tedium of the production line, but they make ideal orators, writers, and thespians—careers that provide them with the variety they crave. Famous people born under the sign of the Twins include painter Paul Gauguin—who fled his native France for Tahiti in a fit of Gemini ennui—financial mogul Donald Trump, rock star Paul McCartney, and television personality Joan Rivers.

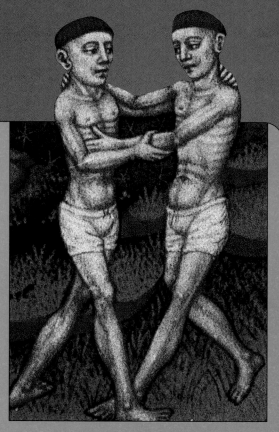

18 MAY

A reverence for twins. *Among the Yoruba people of Nigeria, twins—ibeji—are believed to have powers beyond the normal human measure. Therefore, at this and other times of the year, mothers of twins hold special suppers, with the children as the guests of honor. If one of the twins should die, an effigy like the one below, called an ere ibeji, is created to represent the deceased child at the suppers—and to keep the spirit of the living twin from yearning to follow its soul mate into death.*

19 MAY

New England's dark day. *A sense of doom swept over New England around noon on May 19, 1780, as much of the region was plunged into darkness. Chickens settled down to roost, frogs began their nighttime croaking, and many people concluded that the day of judgment had come. There was no eclipse to account for the darkness. Indeed, no explanation has ever been proved, although the cause may have been a high-altitude pall of wind-borne soot from huge forest fires burning in the West.*

20 MAY

A ghostly moment. *After taking off from New York on May 20, 1927, American aviator Charles Lindbergh flew his single-engine plane, the Spirit of St. Louis, for more than thirty-three hours to reach Paris—the first non-stop solo flight across the Atlantic. Later, Lindbergh told of a strange moment in the trip—an out-of-body experience during which he felt his spirit leave his body and hover above it, connected only by "a strand so tenuous that it could have been severed by a breath."*

21 MAY

Behemoth of the Bay. *Purported sea monsters include Chesapeake Bay's Chessie, videotaped by a Maryland couple on May 21, 1982. Scientists found the image too blurry to identify, but they agreed it seemed to be a large animal.*

The Future's Allure

Much as he is pictured doing in the old etching at right, John Dee sat peering into a crystal ball on May 25, 1581. At first he saw nothing. Then, as he continued to focus on the glassy depths, the ball appeared to cloud up, and in the cloudiness a host of spirits seemed to materialize. Thrilled, Dee was sure he was looking ahead in time.

By the time Dee attempted crystal gazing—or scrying, as this ancient form of prognostication was called—he was one of the most celebrated men in England. He had served for years as Queen Elizabeth's royal astrologer and was personal geographer to famed explorer-navigators Sir Walter Raleigh and Sir Humphrey Gilbert. Dee also enjoyed an illustrious reputation as a mathematician.

But nothing attracted his quick mind more strongly than the occult arts, and he now responded wholeheartedly to their call. He immersed himself in the study of alchemy. He staged séances at which he claimed to channel astral messages and converse with angels. And, convinced of his skill as a scryer, he boldly forecast the future on numerous occasions, once telling a Polish nobleman that he would live forever.

Whether Dee ever attempted to foresee

his own fate is unknown, but it was bleak. Unable to remember everything the spirits told him when they appeared in his crystal ball, Dee employed others to do his scrying while he wrote copious notes. The scryers

turned out to be unscrupulous types, and by 1587 Dee's own star was fading. He eventually retired, telling fortunes in order to eat and gaining little in return except an unenviable reputation as a wizard. He died in 1608.

22 MAY

Unsolved mystery. *On May 22, 415 BC, during a war between Athens and Sparta, Athenians awoke to find the city's many busts of the god Hermes mutilated. The affront to divine power caused panic and a fear of dire consequences that proved warranted. While the identity of the true vandals is still a mystery, Athens's most able general, Alcibiades, was condemned to death after rivals accused him of the sacrilege. He fled to Sparta, where his advice ultimately helped defeat the Athenians.*

23 MAY

Repackaged rituals. *Among pagan feasts absorbed by Christianity were Roman spring festivals (see May 29) that became Rogation Days—three days of prayer preceding Ascension Day. The name changed, but the object was the same: to ask divine blessings for crops and to reinforce awareness of civic and private boundaries. At left, on a Rogation Day in 1934, English officials "beat the bounds"—tap a man's head along a town's limits to impress the boundaries upon citizens.*

24 MAY

Regal farming. *When Cambodia was under royal rule, this date was known as Sacred Furrow Day. To attract heavenly favor to the land and magnify the harvest, members of the royal family put their own backs to the plow and turned over a single sacred furrow.*

25 MAY

The Feast of Weeks. *In its original form as a harvest celebration, the Jewish festival of Shavuoth, or the Feast of Weeks, centered around the offering of two loaves of bread made from the first ripened wheat. Later, Shavuoth became associated with the return of Moses from Mount Sinai and the proclamation of the Ten Commandments. In commemoration of those events, modern-day Jews eat a meal made up of special dairy foods, symbolizing God's promise that his Chosen People would settle in a land "flowing with milk and honey."*

God in the Well

The practice known as well dressing dates from the days when people believed that water, the essential ingredient of life, was inhabited by gods or spirits. These spirits had the dreadful power to cause the water to flow or to withhold it, so people naturally made every effort to honor and seek the favor of these divinities.

To keep their water gods content, the Romans staged an annual festival called the Fontinalia, during which flowers were tossed into springs and wells were decorated with wreaths. The water gods of ancient Britain were apparently a more demanding lot, however: Water sources there were appeased not with flowers but with human self-mutilation.

Later, under the influence of Christianity, wells that had once been sacred to pagans were given the names of saints or the Virgin Mary and became the sites of baptismal ceremonies. Some of these so-called Holy

Wells were also said to have curative powers. Among the more famous of Holy Wells are those surrounding the village of Tissington in Derbyshire, where the practice of well dressing continues today.

According to legend, the local festival was first held in 1350, after the Black Death devastated the population of most of Derbyshire but spared Tissington. Villagers concluded that they had been protected by the purity of their well water. Grateful for what they saw as God's grace, they began decorating the wells with flowers.

Today, Tissington's well-dressing festival is held on Ascension Day, the fortieth day after Easter. A wooden frame is erected at each of the five village wells, then the frame is covered with moist clay. Flowers, leaves, buds, and berries are pressed into the clay to form elaborate designs, and these are usually surmounted by a verse from the Bible. Led by the local clergy and choir, the villagers form a procession to visit each well, reading prayers, singing hymns, and blessing the well water at every stop.

---

26 MAY

Dressing up the water supply. *See above.*

27 MAY

A patron of the paranormal. *This date in 1794 marked the birth of Cornelius Vanderbilt, a shipping and railroad magnate who began his career with a loan of one hundred dollars from his mother. A lifelong sufferer from many ailments, the Commodore, as he was known, retained a number of psychic healers and mediums— one of whom supposedly summoned up the ghost of financial wizard Jim Fisk for a particularly important railroad stocks meeting. In his later years, Vanderbilt is said to have slept with containers of water under his bed, in the apparent belief that the liquid would keep the ghosts away.*

28 MAY

Silencing a UFO report. *On this day in 1965, a pilot flying over Australia contacted ground-control operators, exclaiming that a spherical object had kept pace with his craft for ten minutes before surging ahead. Following this, Australian officials allegedly warned the pilot and ground crew to maintain silence about the sighting. The pilot also claimed film that was confiscated would bear out his allegations.*

29 MAY

A benign Mars. *Mars was not only Rome's war god but also a god of agriculture. Around the end of May, farmers honored Mars's gentler side with feasts that included prayers and purification rites, as well as the sacrifice of a pig, a sheep, and an ox. Before sacrificing the animals, people drove them around the limits of farms and villages (below), partly to imprint on their children where the boundaries lay.*

The Triple Blessing

He was born Siddhartha Gautama in 563 BC, but history knows him as the Buddha, "the enlightened one." Time has cloaked his life in legends, most revolving around three major events: his birth, after what tradition describes as an immaculate conception; his enlightenment, when, having become a wandering ascetic who triumphed over all manner of temptation, the thirty-five-year-old Siddhartha achieved perfect knowledge; and the Buddha's final passage into nirvana, a state of illumination and tranquility that ends the cycle of reincarnation.

According to tradition, these three events occurred on days of a full moon in May. Today, Theravada Buddhists observe this "triple blessing" on the feast of Vesakh, the full-moon day of the sixth lunar month, either April or May. On the eve of the celebrations, followers decorate temples and homes with flowers, streamers, and prayer flags; make offerings of rice, flowers, fruits, coins, and incense; and join processions to nearby temples and statues of the Buddha.

The festivals are not always one-day affairs. Some observe the Triple Blessing on three separate days, most celebrating Buddha's birth sometime in April or May.

30 MAY

Lost seeker. *On May 30, 1925, Briton Percy Fawcett entered the jungle on the Brazil-Bolivia border to seek a fabled lost city. He—and several would-be rescuers—vanished.*

31 MAY

Three holy days in one.
See above.

Green Rituals with Old Roots

Ancient peoples thought trees and other plants em- bodied inexhaustible life, since they burst forth with new green vitality every year. And because the reproduction of food plants was crucial to the humans who fed on them, their fertility was a source of wonder and a subject of great concern.

Each year, when the abundant rebirth of plant life recalled the commonly told stories of the world's creation, of chaos yielding to order and fertility ascending triumphantly over barrenness, people credited the awe-inspiring process not to natural, purely physical forces but to gods, spirits, and the supernatural. Many cultures worshiped the life-giving earth itself, in the form of a great mother goddess such as Cybele, a Mediterranean fertility deity whose fecundity is amply displayed in the stone image above. Vegetation, too, was personified. Corn, for example—born of the earth each spring and falling back into the earth as seed in the autumn, only to be born again the next year—was viewed as the offspring of the Mother Goddess and the paternal god of rain.

Early farmers, believing their seeds would produce good crops only by grace of such superhuman powers, sought favor in the spirit world through rituals that reenacted the cycle of birth, death, and regeneration. In those ceremonies human players ornamented with greenery or the fruits of the harvest often took on the roles of plant spirits.

Annual rituals involving plants are still celebrated all over the world, some as festivals adopted by establishment religions. Christianity, for instance, long ago assimilated a number of European plant ceremonies, imparting a churchly gloss—and often a saint's name—to practices that previously were the domain of pagan priests, gods, sprites, and demons. In such cases the people who participate today may know little or nothing of a ritual's origin, regarding the whole exercise as amusing tradition. But in societies that still live close to the old ways of forest and field, the celebration of plant life continues to evoke real spiritual power.

Personifying spring, a youth grins from within a massive hood of hazel leaves during the Whitsun King procession through the town of Arbesthal, Austria. Now a part of the Christian celebration of the Pentecost, when the Holy Spirit descended on the disciples seven weeks after Christ's resurrection and caused them to speak in tongues, this Whitmonday ceremony was probably originally a Slavic or Teutonic spring fertility rite.

Villagers follow the two Whitsun Kings (below) as they wend their way among Arbesthal's houses and fields. The day includes much singing and dancing and ends with an "auction" of the Whitsun Kings to raise money for local charities. This may be rooted in the ancient practice of demanding food or money for the spirits; failure to contribute invited punishment from the messengers of vegetation.

At winter's end, a wicked spirit named Pust, horned and moss-covered, leads a parade of Yugoslavs clad in winter vegetation. Pust is found guilty of the past year's sins and is replaced by the joyful pair at right above— ivy-clad Brslanast and daisy-decked Marjetica, representing spring.

Jack-in-the-Green (left) is a central character in springtime festivals in Britain and much of Europe. A wickerwork frame covered with green boughs that hide a person within, Jack embodies the idea of new life springing from the cold earth, and the spirit of reviving vegetation.

The Welschkornnarro, or Corn Jester (below), is one of five jesters appearing in pre-Lenten celebrations in the German Black Forest town of Zell. Dressed entirely in corn leaves, he represents opulent harvests past and future. With the other jesters he awakens after a year's slumber, mingles with townspeople for three days, then removes his mask at midnight on Shrove Tuesday. A jester effigy is buried amid weeping and wailing, to sleep like seeds for another year.

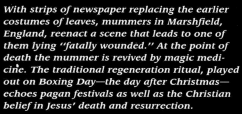

With strips of newspaper replacing the earlier costumes of leaves, mummers in Marshfield, England, reenact a scene that leads to one of them lying "fatally wounded." At the point of death the mummer is revived by magic medicine. The traditional regeneration ritual, played out on Boxing Day—the day after Christmas— echoes pagan festivals as well as the Christian belief in Jesus' death and resurrection.

The Garland King rides in a covering of wildflowers and greenery during the May festival in Castleton, England. His procession stops at six pubs for music and dancing before ending at the village church, where the conical garland is hoisted to the top of the church tower. It is thought that perhaps the Garland King was once a pagan sacrificial victim and that the ceremony practiced today developed as a compromise between Christianity and magic.

Gracefully swinging their huge blossom hats, dancers in Chiyoda, Japan, summon the Shinto god Sanbai-sama to help transplant the young rice shoots. This summer monsoon ritual, called Mibu Ohana-taue, is preserved by the Japanese government as a national "folk-culture asset."

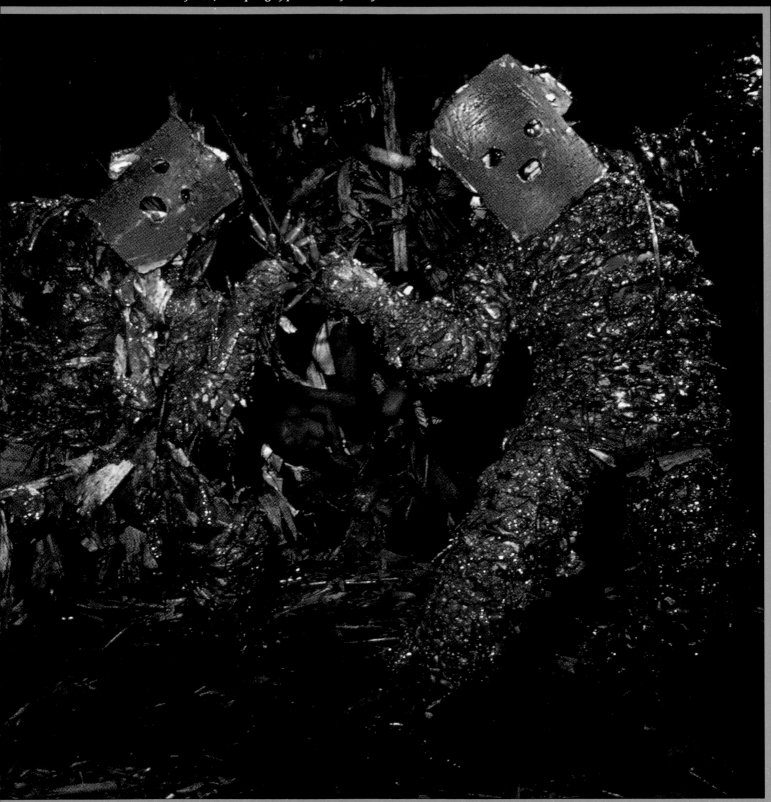

The costumes evoke an ancient era when, they say, settlement was indistinguishable from the wild and women—now fiercely subjugated— roamed at will in the rain forest, wellspring of power and fertility.

Summer

Tradition links June's birthstone, the pearl, with the moon, the sea, and virginity. The jewel supposedly helps to attract admirers and brings business success.

Considered the luckiest of all gems, July's birthstone, the ruby, reportedly attracts good fortune in romance—and wards off bad dreams and unhappiness.

Sardonyx is special to August. The striated red and white stone was once thought to ensure marital happiness and fidelity.

As the exhilarating days of spring lengthen into those of lazy summer, the tempo of daily life slows in many parts of the world to a leisurely crawl that is punctuated by the variety of outdoor festivals and uncanny events described in the pages that follow. Thanks to the enervating temperatures, people show a natural preference for relaxation, restricting work to what is necessary to get by. So little news is generated during this restful time that summer has become known as journalism's "silly season," when reports of usually slighted topics such as unidentified flying objects, sea serpents, or haunted houses are more likely to make the headlines and newscasts. Perhaps it has always been so. Many of the best-known reports of strange events and allegations of paranormal activity throughout history can be traced to occurrences at this time of year.

Only a few threats disturb the even tenor of this calmest of the four seasons. For farmers, the coming crop remains a vulnerable one until the harvest, subject at any moment to drought, flood, wind, or swarming insects. Farmers in Belgium once prayed on Saint Christopher's Day to avert crop-destroying summer tempests; their Japanese counterparts invoke the protection of a rice god. In cities, summer's heat has often bred disease—a threat still warded off in traditional rituals and parades held throughout Europe, Britain, and Japan.

By far the dominant theme of summer, however, is growth in the fields. Rites celebrating the fertility of the crops and the power of the energizing sun are common in June, a fertile month that the Romans named after Juno, goddess of marriage. By tradition, the most magical day of this period comes late in June on Midsummer Eve (which in astronomical terms is summer's beginning, not its midpoint). A wealth of pagan rites once celebrated that date as the longest day and shortest night of the year, and many still exist or have been revived. As harvesting begins in some areas in late July and in August (named after Roman emperors Julius and Augustus), other customs and observances take hold, many celebrating the first fruits of the harvest and the plentiful food that follows. All too soon, however, shortening days mark the end of this easy season, and the languor of summer turns to the industrious labor of fall.

In this medieval woodcut, a priest and his attendants defy all modern notions of conjugal privacy by visiting a newly wed couple as they lie in their bed. The cleric sprinkles the lovers with holy water to ensure the fertility and good fortune of their union.

1 JUNE

The marrying month. *Named after Juno, the Roman goddess of marriage, the month of June was considered by the ancient Romans to be the most auspicious time for weddings. More than fifteen centuries later, the month remains a favorite for nuptials in many Western cultures. Other wedding customs—including the medieval one of blessing the marriage bed (above, left)—owe much to early European beliefs about fertility. The traditional wedding cake, for example, traces its heritage to a time when the bride wore ears of grain to ensure her fertility. The grain gave way to bread and then to wedding cake.*

2 JUNE

Gawai Dayak. *A yearly festival held by the Iban people of Malaysia on the first or second day of June, Gawai Dayak celebrates the gathering of the local harvest. In the huge common rooms of long houses perched high atop stilts in jungle clearings, families gather at midnight as the holiday begins, offering thanks to the gods and invoking their blessing. After a lavish feast complete with rice wine, revelers round off the occasion by selecting the most beautiful man and woman among them as a kind of embodiment of the year's harvest spirit.*

A Bad Day for Birthdays

Long ago, pre-Christian Europeans are thought to have held a festival in early June to mark the death of winter and the birth of summer. With the arrival of Christianity, the official purpose of the June feast changed to celebrating the Pentecost, when the Holy Spirit is said to have descended upon the first apostles, leading them to baptize three thousand new converts in a single day.

Known in Britain as Whitsunday, or

3 JUNE

A seaside ritual. *At about this time of year, worshipers on the Mediterranean island of Cyprus observe the festival of Cataclysmos by praying for the dead and making a special trip to the sea. After sprinkling each other with seawater—said to be especially blessed this day—celebrants play traditional water games and perform a dance that requires participants to balance as many as six glasses of water on their heads. Although celebrated as a Christian holiday, Cataclysmos may have evolved from a far more ancient rite, held to mark the end of a flood supposedly sent by Zeus to destroy humankind for its wickedness.*

4 JUNE

Whitsunday. *See below.*

5 JUNE

Dancing for a good harvest. *Throughout the spring and summer months, the Pueblo peoples of New Mexico perform traditional corn dances like the one pictured above, dedicated to the Rain People and the Earth Mothers and meant to ensure a good harvest and a blessing on the earth. Shaking traditional rattles, men and women dressed in white and adorned with feathers mingle in the solemn ritual.*

6 JUNE

Return of the ancestors. *Early in June, the Yoruba people of Nigeria honor the spirits of their ancestors with a week-long festival. According to Yoruba belief, these otherworldly entities, known as the Egungun, control the fates of the living and must be properly honored and venerated. During the festival some villagers offer food and gifts to the spirits, while Egungun impersonators like the one pictured below dance through the streets. At times, participants believe, the living dancers find themselves possessed by the long-dead Egungun spirits.*

sometimes simply Whit, for the white vestments that baptismal candidates wear on this occasion, the Church festival has long retained many of its pagan associations—including goblet-wielding fertility figures like those seen at left in full vegetation regalia at a German gathering. One hallowed British belief has it that a child born on Whitsunday is doomed either to kill or to be killed. To fool the fates, parents of old held mock funerals for Whitsunday babies. For those not born on the day, however, Whitsunday may be a lucky time. According to one belief, whatever one asks for as the sun rises on Whitsunday will be granted. A fine and fair Whitsunday is believed to augur a good harvest. Because the feast welcomes the newborn summer, moreover, it has long been considered unlucky to venture out on this day without wearing something new.

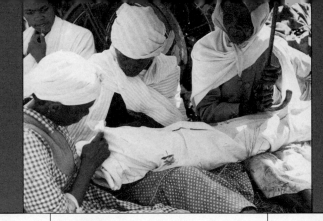

7 JUNE

Visit to the inner sanctum. *On this date in ancient Rome began the festival of Vestalia, which honored Vesta, goddess of the hearth. During this time Vesta's shrine—ordinarily forbidden ground to all but her attendant vestal virgins—was opened to married women for eight days. After walking to the temple barefoot, the matrons made offerings of food to the goddess, who they believed guarded their homes and household fires. On June 15, the housewives returned home, and the shrine was once again off-limits until Vestalia came again.*

8 JUNE

Rice festivals. *As rice seedlings are transplanted to the paddies in early June, many Japanese villages hold ceremonies to ask the blessing of the rice god on the crop. In a typical rite, women planters in traditional kimonos recite prayers and light rice-straw fires to lure the god from his mountain home. Then, moving rhythmically to the music of drummers and pipers, they stoop and plant in near-choreographic unison (below) until the paddy is filled. At day's end, according to tradition, the god goes home to await his worshipers' next call.*

9 JUNE

Turning over the dead. *Every few summers—and sometimes more often—the Malagasy highlanders of Madagascar open their family tombs and exhume the bodies of dead relatives in a ceremony called famadihana, literally "turning over the dead." After wrapping the corpses in silk shrouds (above), joyful family members carry the remains around the graveyard or through the streets before reinterring their burdens. Because they believe the dead still live, the Malagasy often call upon their ancestors for help. This is the only day, however, that the dead physically return.*

10 JUNE

A victim of the witch mania. *On this day in 1692, Bridget Bishop became the first of nineteen men and women to be hanged for witchcraft in Salem, Massachusetts, in conjunction with the famous trials there.*

Beware the Juggernauts

Once every June, tens of thousands of Hindu pilgrims flock to the city of Puri on India's eastern coast for a joyous festival honoring the god Jagannath, a benevolent incarnation of Vishnu, lord of creation. The day before the festivities begin, attendants at Jagannath's temple adorn three huge statues of the god, his brother, and his sister with crowns of flowers and golden robes. They then transfer the figures to three enormous chariots, or cars, lined up outside. At forty-five feet high, Jagannath's splendid car is the largest. It rests on sixteen wooden wheels, each about seven feet in diameter.

The next morning, thousands of the faithful gather in the temple courtyard. At a signal from Jagannath's priests, they take up thick ropes attached to the sacred cars and begin drawing them through Puri's main street to a building known as Jagannath's garden house. Although their goal lies only a mile or so away, the journey takes up most of the day. Immense, noisy crowds like the one shown here throng the route, and enthusiastic worshipers constantly surge toward the sacred, cloth-draped structures, hoping to be blessed by a turn at the ropes.

When the carts and their monumental occupants at last reach the garden house, the carts are parked and the statues taken

11 JUNE

Sighting a ghost ship. *In the early morning hours on this date in 1881, a wakeful pair of British princes—one of them the future King George V—saw a strange ship bathed in a red glow glide by their naval vessel as they sailed near the Australian coast. Others aboard also witnessed the phenomenon, which the shocked group identified as the legendary Flying Dutchman, a spectral ship that was doomed to sail the sea for eternity because its captain had cursed God.*

12 JUNE

Washing away bad luck. *Like their counterparts in Japan (see June 8), many Korean rice farmers perform an ancient ritual before transplanting the precious rice seedlings into place. To ensure an abundant crop, these farmers wash their hair in a stream, hoping that any ill fortune that might be clinging to them will be carried away with the current.*

13 JUNE

Birth of a modern witch. *On this date in 1884 was born Gerald Gardner, who became a British customs inspector and self-proclaimed witch. With his 1954 book Witchcraft Today, Gardner greatly influenced the modern witchcraft and neopagan movements.*

A lifelong love of magic. *Irish poet William Butler Yeats, born on this date in 1865, said he could not have written some of his works "if I had not made magic my constant study." His interest in magic led Yeats to join the secretive Order of the Golden Dawn.*

14 JUNE

Festival of Jagannath. *See below.*

inside. There they remain for seven days, while the pilgrims indulge in feasting and riotous dancing. On the eighth day, Jagannath and his siblings return to his temple in the same vehicles by which they left it.

It has been reported by foreign observers that in the past, some pilgrims, driven to a frenzy of religious excitement, threw themselves beneath the wheels of Jagannath's car and were crushed to death. Undoubtedly, there were accidents in which unfortunates fell into a chariot's path. Because of such incidents, the English word juggernaut—a variant of the god Jagannath's name—has come to mean any inexorable force that crushes everything in its path, a peculiar association for a god meant to help, rather than slaughter, humankind.

15 JUNE

Corpus Christi. *On the second Thursday after Pentecost, the Roman Catholic and Orthodox churches celebrate Corpus Christi. This festival honors the mystical rite of communion, during which Christians consume the Body of Christ—in Latin, Corpus Christi—in the form of consecrated bread. As missionaries introduced Christianity into Peru, Bolivia, and other parts of the old Incan empire, this Church feast largely replaced traditional Incan solstice rituals. The result was a mixture of Incan and Catholic elements that persists today, as crowds parade consecrated bread through streets carpeted with flower petals arranged in geometric figures.*

16 JUNE

Obituary for the human soul. *On this date in 1975, the New York Times obituary page carried a short article announcing that a search for the human soul had come to an inconclusive end. As explained in the story, an eccentric Arizona miner named James Kidd had disappeared one day in 1949, leaving behind roughly $174,000 and a will requesting that the money be used to obtain "scientific proof of a soul of the human body which leaves at death." The American Society for Psychical Research, which took up the challenge, proved unable to demonstrate the existence of any human soul—an outcome that inspired the newspaper obituary.*

17 JUNE

The cleansing lily. *In a centuries-old purification ritual, the people of the Japanese city of Nara collect thousands of lily stalks from a nearby mountain at about this time and take them to a temple, where the flowers are blessed by seven young women in white robes. The next morning, a Shinto priest lays a large lily bouquet at the altar, after which the seven maidens wave lily stalks in a traditional dance designed to drive away the evils of the rainy season. At the end of the performance, attendees transport a large lily-filled float through the city streets to purify the air.*

18 JUNE

Dragon Boat Festival. *See above and below.*

Dragon Boats Searching for a Drowned Poet

Near the summer solstice, the Chinese people celebrate a holiday known to Westerners as the Dragon Boat Festival. According to legend, the festival commemorates the death in the year 278 BC of Qu Yuan, a Chinese statesman and poet. As the story is told, Qu Yuan deliberately flung himself into a river in sorrow at the corruption of his home state of Chu. Villagers rushed to their boats in a vain effort to save him. Rice also played a role in the rescue effort; some accounts say searchers threw rice dumplings in the river to distract the dragons and evil spirits lurking in the water, while other stories have it that the rice was a tribute to the soul of the martyred poet.

Ever since, as the story goes, boat races have been held annually to commemorate the futile search for the dead hero; spectators eat rice cakes in memory of the rice poured overboard by the searchers. Crews row large, dragon-shaped boats like the one pictured above.

According to some researchers, however, the dragon design of the vessels suggests that the boat races may actually predate Qu Yuan's death by several centuries. The races, they say, may have begun as an ancient summer solstice ritual intended to propitiate the river dragons, which in Chinese tradition are benevolent guardians who bring rain. To please the dragon gods, the boats were made to resemble them. Later, the ancient rites—and the traditional rice cakes—may have been integrated with Qu Yuan's story to produce the festival observed today.

Cancer: June 22-July 22

Cancer, first of the three water signs in the zodiac, begins today. Ruled by the moon, Cancerians are attuned—say astrologers—to such natural cycles as gestation and motherhood. And Cancer's symbol, the crab, represents the sea, where life began.

Like the crab, Cancerians hide a vulnerable interior under a tough shell. They are instinctively compassionate and nurturing, but on the outside, a brittle carapace shields them against a potentially hostile world. Quick to take offense, they swiftly retreat into their shells when their feelings are hurt.

Influenced by the moon and its tides, Cancerians are often moody and restless, melancholy and introverted one moment, cheerful and enthusiastic the next. They usually harbor a persistent fear of the future.

Cancer natives revel in the comfort and stability of family and tradition, and their homes are beloved havens from which they venture into the world. Accordingly, women born under this moon sign are likely to embrace the roles of wife and mother, and Cancerian men, who are deeply attached to their own mothers throughout life, seek a domestic life of harmony and emotional security. Natives of both sexes often feel a lifelong link to childhood and memories.

Indeed Cancerians boast great powers of memory. They are also uncannily perceptive and sensitive to their environment and to other people's needs. Famous people born under the sign include comedian Bill Cosby, tennis player Arthur Ashe, actress Meryl Streep, and Diana, Princess of Wales.

19 JUNE

When the Emperor calls. *This day marks the beginning of a week-long celebration in Brazil, the Feast of the Holy Ghost. In rural communities, one wealthy farmer is chosen as Emperor of the festivities. He plans the huge event but relies upon the contributions of others to carry it off. Months before the occasion, the so-called Emperor and a group of musicians travel through the countryside, stopping at each farm and requesting through an age-old musical entreaty a pledge of livestock or grain for the feast. On the day of the event, the farmers gather to fulfill their promises, and the celebration begins.*

20 JUNE

A mystical seal. *On June 20, 1782, Charles Thomson's design for the U.S. seal was approved. The reverse (below) featured a pyramid and an all-seeing eye, two mysterious symbols cherished by the Freemasons.*

21 JUNE

Solstice rites, East and West. *On or about this date comes the Northern Hemisphere's summer solstice, an event rife with ancient meaning that occurs when the sun attains its highest point in the heavens and begins its inevitable decline toward the darkness of winter. In England, modern Druids mark the solstice with sunrise rituals at Stonehenge (below); in Japan, a solstice festival known as Geshi emphasizes prayers for protection against the heat and disease of summer.*

22 JUNE

The sun enters the sign of Cancer. *See above.*

A Peruvian Indian raises a chalice in offering to the sun during a contemporary reenactment of an ancient Incan ritual held at the Southern Hemisphere's winter solstice.

23 JUNE

Midsummer Eve. *See below.*

24 JUNE

Prayer for the sun's return. *On this date, near the time of the winter solstice south of the equator, the Incas of Peru once held a sun-god festival known as Inti Raymi, shown being reenacted above. Priests foretold the future from the entrails of freshly killed llamas.*

First flying saucers. *While flying over the Cascade Mountains on this day in 1947, businessman Kenneth Arnold spotted several airborne objects he described as "flying saucers." In the years that followed, other flying saucers were reported in thousands of incidents around the world.*

25 JUNE

Visions of a disaster. *On this day in 1876, General George Custer and all his men died in a battle against Sioux Indians at the Little Bighorn River in Montana. At least two people had premonitions of the bloodbath. Three weeks before, Sitting Bull, a Sioux medicine man, saw a vision of many soldiers attacking his camp. Then Elizabeth Custer, the general's wife, had a strange experience while watching her husband and his troops ride off. She saw them reflected in the sky—which she took as a sign that they were on their way to heaven.*

26 JUNE

Revenge of the Pied Piper. *On this day in 1284, a real Pied Piper is said to have visited the German town of Hamelin. There, he reportedly led the resident children to their demise in a sealed cave by playing alluring melodies on his pipe. The piper had previously rid Hamelin of its rats, but he had never been paid for the good deed, so he stole the town's children as retaliation.*

The Magic of Midsummer Eve

Perhaps no other time of the year is so pregnant with mystical possibilities as Midsummer Eve. Celebrated since early Christian times on June 23, the eve of Saint John's Day, the rituals of Midsummer Eve have changed very little from the pagan celebrations that once marked the summer solstice that occurs a few days before.

Chief among these is the lighting of bonfires, a practice once found—and, in some cases, still observed—in Britain, Europe, South America, and North Africa. Such blazes were probably kindled originally to strengthen the spirit of the weakening sun god and ensure his eventual return to full glory. According to traditional belief, the flames themselves had a number of magical qualities. Dancing around the fire or leaping through the flames *(right)* was thought to bring good luck and to keep evil spirits at bay, and farmers sometimes drove their cattle around the fire to banish pestilence and disease. In some Welsh towns, revelers set wheels or barrels ablaze and sent them rolling downhill to carry away ill fortune. In eighteenth-century Ireland, townsfolk lit torches from the bonfires, then ran with them through the village to purify the air, which was likely to be infected with malign influences on this night.

For on Midsummer Eve—as Shakespeare suggested in *A Midsummer Night's Dream*—the barrier between the visible realm of the living and the invisible world of ghosts and fairies was thought to stretch so thin that otherworldly creatures might easily penetrate it. Fire was not the only precaution against such visitors. The golden flower known as St.-John's-wort, for instance, was believed to ward off the devil and other evil spirits—and to protect the eyes from the glare of the bonfires. Fern seeds, too, were considered a sovereign guard against Midsummer Eve witchcraft. They also provided white magic, enabling a maiden to see a Midsummer apparition of her future husband; she had only to scatter the seed at midnight and peek over her shoulder. Myriad other love divinations were linked to Midsummer Eve, which is still considered by modern witches to be the best time to gather magic plants.

Explosion over Siberia

On this morning in 1908, a massive, fiery—and still unidentified—object from outer space burst into the sky over the remote Siberian region of Tunguska. As it collided with Earth's atmosphere, it created a blast unrivaled in human history, generating a scorching wind that flattened and burned twelve hundred square miles of forest into charred stumps like those shown here.

The cause of the cataclysm remains a mystery among scientists and laypeople alike. Astronomers generally incline to the theory that the Tunguska object could have been a comet or an asteroid that exploded as it hit the atmosphere, generating a wave of infernal heat but no impact crater. UFO researchers, however, have speculated that it was a massive alien spaceship—deliberately steered to the remote woodlands of Siberia to avoid striking any human population centers. Whether UFO, asteroid, or comet, the object was undeniably and impressively large: Calculations show that whatever hit Tunguska measured 300 feet across and weighed as much as a million tons.

27 JUNE

The magic of the dance. *At about this time of year, many Plains Indian tribes perform a Sun Dance to honor the burning summer sun. Among the magical items associated with such dances is a special Crow totem that is adorned with bird feathers. If it is held during a Sun Dance by the relative of a murder victim, the totem is said to reveal the identity of the killer.*

28 JUNE

A dream of assassination. *Early in the morning on this date in 1914, Hungarian bishop Monsignor de Lanyi reportedly had a dream foretelling the event that precipitated World War I: the assassination of his former pupil, Austrian archduke Francis Ferdinand. In the dream he saw not only the archduke but also Ferdinand's wife being shot to death as they rode in a carriage. Later, the bishop received a cable confirming that archduke and archduchess were dead, murdered that day under circumstances eerily similar to Lanyi's alleged dream.*

29 JUNE

Bawming the Thorn. *In a late June ceremony that may have arisen from pagan tree worship rituals, the people of Appleton, England, ceremoniously decorate—or "bawm"—an enormous hawthorn tree that grows in the center of town. After marching in procession to the tree, villagers deck its branches with flowers, flags, and ribbons. When the venerable tree has been suitably adorned, Appleton's children dance under its aged boughs.*

30 JUNE

A gargantuan blast. *See above.*

Tribute to the Serpent Gods

Since ancient times, the Indians and Nepalese have feared and worshiped snakes, which they consider the earthly relations of snake gods known as Nagas. Said to inhabit the world's nether regions, the Nagas can bring or withhold rain, cure or cause disease, grant good or bad fortune, and prevent or inflict death by snakebite. During the festival of Naga Panchami, the people of Nepal and India commemorate a promise given by the Nagas on this date many centuries ago.

The promise was made, according to legend, after a poor farmer accidentally killed three baby snakes while tilling his field. Maddened by grief, the mother serpent entered his house and killed him, his wife, and their two sons with her venomous fangs. When she turned to the remaining child, a daughter, the quick-thinking girl set a bowl of milk before her. Pleased, the mother snake not only spared the girl's life, but granted her anything she wished. The daughter asked simply that her family be returned to life and that the Nagas agree to refrain from killing anyone else on that day. The snake acceded and slithered away.

On Naga Panchami, worshipers mark the anniversary of that agreement by displaying snake images and placing offerings of milk, grain, or other food at snake holes. In some Indian villages, live serpents are paraded through town in processions like the one shown here. To avoid a repetition of the original accident, plowing and digging are forbidden on this day.

1 JULY

Serpent festival. *See above.*

2 JULY

A crashed UFO? *On this night in 1947, an unidentified flying object crashed in the desert near Roswell, New Mexico. Official investigators (below) called it a weather balloon. But unverified reports later surfaced that four aliens—one alive and well—were found in the wreckage.*

3 JULY

Green corn dance. *At this time of year, the Seminole Indians of Florida perform a "green corn dance" to honor the new corn crop. The men of the tribe then eat the first corn, marking the start of the Seminole new year.*

4 JULY

Keeping death at bay. *This day in 1826 was the fiftieth anniversary of the birth of the United States. John Adams and Thomas Jefferson, the second and third presidents of the new nation, died that day. Both men had suffered serious illnesses for some time, yet relatives reported that they had apparently willed themselves to live to see this milestone in the history of the country they had helped to shape.*

A pair of festively painted bullocks draw a cart bearing pots of snakes through the streets of a village in India during a Naga Panchami parade. The man dressed in white at the rear of the cart displays one of the sacred reptiles while controlling its movements with a stick.

This modern rendition of a traditional Japanese folk cutout depicts the legendary Tanabata lovers returning to each other on the backs of magpies. According to the tale, the birds took pity upon the two heavenly beings, who were separated by a raging river, and bridged the intervening torrent with their own bodies.

5 JULY

A case for the exorcist. On this date in 1906, a sixteen-year-old South African schoolgirl named Clara Germana Celle gave her priest, Father Erasmus Hoerner, a hand-written pact she had supposedly made with the devil. Over the next two months, the formerly quiet girl reportedly exhibited many classic signs of demonic possession, including barking like an animal, struggling with invisible foes, levitating, and speaking in the voice of Satan. Not until a team of priests and nuns performed the rite of exorcism two months later was Germana rid of her tormentor.

6 JULY

Victims of a kingly killer. On July 6, 1933, two small skeletons that had been discovered in the Tower of London more than two centuries earlier underwent a modern technical examination. As had long been suspected, they were identified as almost certainly the remains of two princes—one the rightful king of England—consigned to the fortress by their uncle Richard III in 1483. Rumored to have been murdered by Richard's orders, the boys reportedly haunt the ancient prison's so-called Bloody Tower.

7 JULY

Tanabata Star Festival. Each year on this day, Japanese families mark the reunion of two celestial lovers (above) by tying personal pleas and children's writing samples to bamboo fronds. Tradition holds that the prayers will be answered and the children's writing will be improved.

8 JULY

Parading for health. On this day in the Portuguese town of Tomar, 600 girls parade through the streets balancing on their heads tall flower-bedecked pillars made of bread (below). Carefully preserved, the bread is said to prevent illness for the rest of the year.

A Welcome Visit from the Dead

Every summer, according to Japanese belief, the spirits of the dead return to mingle with the living during the three-day Bon Festival. Many people make special trips home for the holiday so that all family members—both the ancestors and their living descendants—may participate in the happy reunion.

To prepare, families clean household shrines and the graves of relatives, then fill both sites with offerings of herbs, flowers, and food. On the evening of July 13, family members gather at graveside to greet ancestral spirits and escort them home, illuminating the night with lanterns and torches like those in the cemetery scene at right.

That night and for the rest of the festival, families feast and celebrate, laying a place at meals for their deceased houseguests and including the departed in all conversation. Most also spend some time in solemn meditation, acknowledging the debt each owes to the ancestors. Outdoors, revelers gather at night in parks or squares to join in the traditional Bon dance, a gladsome affair intended to greet and comfort the dead souls.

As the Bon Festival draws to an end, the living hosts light farewell fires and set out lanterns to illuminate for the spirits the way home to their graves. In some areas, families also launch miniature boats equipped with tiny lanterns to cheer the spirits and speed their return to the other side.

9 JULY

A dog's psychic summons. *On this night in 1904, English adventure story writer Henry Rider Haggard awoke uttering preternatural moans. He had been dreaming, he said, that his daughter's black retriever, Bob, lay dead near a body of water. In the morning they determined that the dog was indeed missing, and three days later Bob was found dead, floating near a small dam. Haggard believed that his uncanny dream had resulted from a psychic cry for help from the animal.*

10 JULY

A new dress for a goddess. *Every year at this time, ancient Athenians celebrated Panathenaea, a festival for Athena, their patron goddess. Once every four years—on this day, the sixth of the celebration—they presented Athena with a brilliant new robe. First they paraded it through the city streets, then they mounted the Acropolis, where priests draped the garment over the statue of the goddess at the Shrine of Athena.*

11 JULY

A puzzling parade of giants. *On the Sunday following July 5 in Douai, France, the local Fête de Gayant festival concludes with a parade of wickerwork giants (below). No one knows the origin or purpose of this ceremony, which remains a mystery even to those who participate.*

12 JULY

A most fortuitous day. *Legend tells that the archangel Gabriel revealed this day as one of the luckiest of the year. On July 12, healing, planting, house building, traveling, and even waging war will supposedly proceed without a hitch. Children born on this date will be wealthy, and students who commence their work today will become great scholars. Also, anyone who begins a new job on July 12 will enjoy great success.*

13 JULY

Japanese Bon Festival. *See above.*

14 JULY

Mystifying wheat circles. *On this night in 1988, five circular impressions emerged in a wheat field near Silbury Hill, a large mound of earth created by ancient Britons in southwest England. A few days later, five more circles appeared in the same field (below), and within eight weeks, forty-six other circles showed up in fields within seven miles. Although crop circles elsewhere have proved to be hoaxes, these remain unexplained.*

15 JULY

Saint Swithin's Day. *On this day is celebrated the feast of Saint Swithin, a bishop of Winchester who died in AD 862. Legend has it that tenth-century monks tried to move his body to a place of honor but were prevented by forty days of rain. Ever since, the weather on Swithin's day has been said to forecast whether the next forty days will be fair or rainy.*

16 JULY

Voodoo pilgrims of Saut d'Eau. *At this time in Haiti, thousands of the voodoo faithful seek healing or good health with a pilgrimage to the holy waters of Saut d'Eau, a waterfall (below) where Erzulie Freda, the voodoo spirit of love, is said to have appeared twice in the 1800s.*

17 JULY

Spears that defeated a plague. *In the summer of AD 869, according to Japanese legend, the Emperor Seiwa successfully rid the city of Kyoto of an epidemic by displaying sixty-six spears in front of his imperial shrine. So grateful was Seiwa to the gods for the end of the pestilence that he began parading the spears through the streets every year, a custom continued to this day in the city's July 17 Gion Festival. The spears now travel through the streets in large sapling-topped shrines like those above. Dozens of musicians accompany the grand procession, which is led by a boy dressed as a Shinto priest.*

18 JULY

A holiday for carpenters. *The patron saint of Chinese carpenters and builders, Lu Pan was born on this day in 606 BC, according to Hong Kong tradition. Tales of the skilled carpenter's feats are legendary: One account has it that he repaired the very pillars of heaven when they were in danger of collapse. To honor his memory, Hong Kong carpenters and builders pay a special visit to Lu Pan's temple at noon on his birthday. During the rest of the year, workmen offer feasts to the revered carpenter whenever a new building is completed.*

19 JULY

Festival of Isis. *Worshiped as one of the nine major Egyptian deities, the goddess Isis was also the object of a Roman cult, which on this day held a festival in her honor. The celebration, observed in the city of Rome well into the fourth century AD, commemorated the annual flooding of the Nile River, which deposited fertile soil along the riverbank, turning what would otherwise have been desert land into a fecund planting ground. To the ancients, the rich inundation was nothing short of a miracle that was provided by Isis, the benevolent universal mother.*

20 JULY

Help for expectant mothers. *On July 20 is celebrated the Christian feast of Saint Margaret, an Italian virgin who was martyred in AD 278 for refusing to marry a wicked Eastern potentate. Her girdle was at one time preserved in a Paris church, where women go on this day to pray to Saint Margaret to ease the pains of childbirth.*

Leo: July 23-August 22

Symbolized by the Lion, the king of beasts, Leo begins its reign of zodiacal influence on July 23. Proud, confident, and daring, Leos tend to view themselves at the center of things, like their ruling planet, the Sun. (Because the ancients viewed the sun as a planet, astrologers still call it one.) Leo is also associated with fire, a dynamic and transforming element that, along with the Sun, imparts great vitality and energy to people born under the sign.

Indeed the Sun's influence, according to astrologers, gives Leos a keen sense of their own strength and consciousness. They are likely to be leaders—or at least to see themselves that way. For despite their tremendous potential for honesty, generosity, and courage, their powerful egos can lead them into an exaggerated sense of self that engenders vanity, greed, and tyranny. Leos must learn to temper their strong will with social responsibility if they are to fulfill the noble goals of which they are capable.

Even the most mature Leos, however, still crave recognition and admiration. Accordingly, they stand out in occupations that enable them to be the center of attention, such as politics and the performing arts. Comedian Lucille Ball, actor Robert Redford, and singer Madonna were all born under the sign of the Lion.

Faithful and giving, Leos make wonderful partners—when they can curb their tendency to dominate. They express themselves sincerely, loathing hypocrisy, and they savor all the richness that life holds. Their unbridled enthusiasm for the world's finer things, however, inclines them toward extravagance: Astrologers have dubbed Leo one of the most spendthrift signs of the zodiac.

21 JULY

The Mayan New Year. *For the Maya of Central America, each day, year, decade, century, and millennium had its own god. To determine which deity was in control, the Maya maintained a solar calendar of 365 days and a sacred calendar of 260 days, a system depicted in part on the glyph below. Every fifty-second solar New Year, which might fall in any season, was considered dangerous, for the gods might then abandon their burdens and bring time to a dead stop.*

22 JULY

A monster in Loch Ness. *The first recorded modern sighting of the Loch Ness monster—allegedly pictured in the 1977 photograph below—took place on this date in 1930. Three boys said they were fishing from a boat when an animal more than twenty feet long rushed toward them and then veered off. Since then, the monster has been glimpsed by thousands of people.*

23 JULY

A historic séance. *On this date in 1855, British poets Robert and Elizabeth Barrett Browning attended a séance conducted by the famed medium Daniel Dunglas Home at the residence of London solicitor John Rymer and his wife. As the evening wore on, the Brownings reportedly witnessed a number of mysterious occurrences, including the manifestation of several disembodied hands—one pair of which placed a wreath of clematis on Mrs. Browning's head.*

24 JULY

A monk's lofty mortifications. *A fourth-century Cilician teenager experienced a vision in which he had become an ascetic. Accordingly, the young man joined a monastery. However, he practiced such severe self-abnegation that he was asked to leave. Undaunted, he embarked upon a life of solitary austerity that eventually led to his living atop high pillars as a means of escaping humanity. Though these aeries afforded him no shelter, he rarely descended. Remarkably, he lived to the age of sixty-nine and is thought to have died on this day. He was canonized and is known as Saint Simeon Stylites—from the Greek stylos, for pillar.*

Return to the Underworld

Every year, the Hopi of northeastern Arizona observe a cycle of dances and ceremonies in honor of the kachinas, living supernatural beings believed to aid the tribe in its eternal quest for survival. The kachinas are said to have accompanied the ancestors of the Hopi people when they first emerged from the underworld onto the surface of the earth.

Although the subsequent fate of the kachinas varies from story to story, one legend holds that the kachinas deserted their people when the Hopi began to take for granted the blessings they received. Before the kachinas returned to the underworld,

This Hopi doll represents the Hemis kachina, a spirit that brings mature corn to the people. Although the Hopi tribe is matriarchal, the men are the exclusive conduits for the kachina spirits. Accordingly, they create effigies such as this one to give to their female relatives as a means of sharing the kachinas' power.

however, they taught a few faithful young men how to perform some of the rituals. If the details of the ceremonies were rigidly observed by men with good and pure hearts, then the spirits would return to earth to possess the worshipers. The vital blessings of rain and well-being would follow.

The Niman dance held at about this time of year marks the end of just such a visit from the kachinas, an annual affair that begins six months earlier in February. At that time, Hopi villages throughout the arid mesa hold a special celebration to welcome the kachinas back to earth. Other ceremonies are performed over the next several months, as men wearing kachina costumes and masks participate in group dances that begin at sunrise and end at sunset, interspersed with prayers for rain and a good harvest. Small kachina figures like the one at left also play a role in the rites. As the sacred cycle culminates, participants perform the final Niman dance as an elaborate farewell to the kachinas on their return to the spirit world.

25 JULY

A saint's pagan heritage. *July 25 is the feast of Saint Christopher. Today's Catholics know the saint as the patron of travelers, but European worshipers of a thousand years ago may have thought of him quite differently. In those days, when early Christians were challenging the beliefs of older polytheistic religions, many peasants fused two faiths into one. In the Flemish parts of Belgium, for instance, they transferred the powers of Thor, god of thunder, rain, and farming, to Christopher. They prayed to the saint on this day as they once had to the thunder god—for protection of their crops against storm-wrought destruction.*

26 JULY

Birth of Jung. *One of the most influential psychiatrists of the twentieth century, Carl Gustav Jung was born on this date in 1875 in a small Swiss village. A student of Sigmund Freud, Jung is best known for his controversial theory that buried deep down in each person's psyche is a vast, inherited repository of images and impulses that Jung called the collective unconscious. In part because of his work on this shared reservoir of ideas, Jung was fascinated by paranormal topics all of his life, among them alchemy, mediumship, and witchcraft.*

27 JULY

Pantaleon's seven lives. *Today marks the feast of Saint Pantaleon, a fourth-century Venetian doctor who foiled six attempts on his life. His executioners—who reportedly sought to kill him simply because he failed to charge his patients for his services—tried burning, drowning, submersion in liquid lead, attacks by wild beasts, putting him to the sword, and breaking him on the wheel, all without success. Only their seventh torture, decapitation, was able to end Pantaleon's life.*

28 JULY

Raksha Bandhan, or Narial Purnima. *Siblings in northern India celebrate this holiday at the end of July and the beginning of August. As a sign of familial unity, the women tie rakshis—amulets or woven strips of colorful yarn—around their brothers' wrists. In return, the brothers give gifts to their sisters and promise to protect them. On this day as well, many believers honor Varuna, the Vedic god of the sea, by throwing coconuts into the ocean. For this reason, Raksha Bandhan is also known as Narial Purnima, or "Coconut Full-Moon."*

A Rite for the Passing of Summer

Though still seasonally hot, the month of August signals summer's demise with its shortening days and lengthening nights. The ancient Celts marked this time with a festival called Lugnasadh, in honor of Lug, the god of light and of the declining sun *(right).* Lugnasadh also celebrated the early harvest.

When the Christian feast of Loaf Mass, or Lammas, took Lugnasadh's place, similar themes prevailed. Until the 1100s, early grain was baked into loaves offered at mass on this day. Another Lammas rite owed even more to pagan roots: Well into the mid-1900s, Scottish farmers ceremonially cut handfuls of corn to wheel around their heads in praise of the harvest god. In another rite, farmers threw sickles in the air. From the position of the fallen sickles, it was believed that they could predict who would marry, grow ill, or die before Lammas came again.

Lammas was also a time to celebrate the harvest of wild foods. In medieval times, a maiden was dressed in white and seated on a hilltop, perhaps representing a long-past spirit of the wood. Villagers climbed the slope in a procession and laid offerings of blackberries, acorns, and crab apples in her lap. A dance and a procession home followed.

While Lammas is still celebrated in some British country churches, Lugnasadh has enjoyed a revival in recent years. Observed by present-day Wiccans as one of eight annual sabbats, Lugnasadh commemorates the first fruits of the harvest, the witches' closeness to the earth, and their oneness with all life.

In this modern illustration of an ancient Celtic myth, Lug—the god of light who is celebrated at Lugnasadh—slings a stone at the deadly Cyclopean eye of his grandfather in a symbolic battle between the forces of good and evil.

29 JULY

Martha and the dragon. *For generations, the French city of Tarascon has held a festival on this day in honor of Saint Martha of Bethany. Legend has it that the city was built on the spot where the saint captured a dragon called Tarasque by binding him fast with her girdle. To commemorate that feat, a dragon float like the one below is carried through Tarascon; onlookers touch the dragon to gain good luck.*

30 JULY

An adopted patron. *On this day, the Micmac Indians of Nova Scotia paddle their canoes to an island in the middle of a lake that has been sacred since pre-Christian times. They pitch birch bark wigwams on the shore and camp there for several days, performing a year's worth of marriages and christenings. But they also honor the Catholic Saint Ann, introduced to them by missionaries two hundred years ago.*

31 JULY

A medium is born. *Influential mystic and medium Helena Petrovna Blavatsky (below) was born in the Ukraine on this date in 1831. Blavatsky credited entities she called the "spirit masters" with writing her classic text Isis Unveiled.*

1 AUGUST

Britain's Lammas rites. *See above.*

2 AUGUST

A shy lady's bold ride. *In the eleventh century, according to medieval chroniclers, Lady Godiva of Coventry exasperated her rich husband by pleading that he help the town's poor. He told his bashful wife he would—only if she rode naked through town. As visualized above in a nineteenth-century painting, Godiva took up the challenge. Miraculously, she rode unobserved— some say because grateful townfolk stayed indoors. Her chastened husband fulfilled his pledge, and she acquired a kind of immortality. In sporadic celebrations held on this day for centuries, Coventry has paraded a young woman—sometimes naked, sometimes garbed— through town on horseback.*

3 AUGUST

Banishing the sandman. *On this day in rural Japan, people begin the harvest season with a ritual called Aomori Nebuta. Villagers promenade huge wire-and-bamboo effigies painted with intense facial expressions through the streets, believing that this action will drive away sleep: The farmers need to be wide awake in order to perform the hard labor of harvesting.*

4 AUGUST

A healing Scottish loch. *Every August until the mid-1800s, Scotland's lame, sick, impotent, and mentally ill flocked to Loch-mo-Naire (below), a lake famed for its healing power. Gathering on the shore at midnight, the ailing pilgrims drank some of the water, then stripped off their clothes and walked backward into the loch, immersing themselves three times. The visitors paid Loch-mo-Naire by flinging silver coins into its watery depths.*

5 AUGUST

UFOs on film. *On this date in 1950, baseball manager Nick Mariana of Great Falls, Montana, was inspecting the home field before a game when he was surprised by a flash in the sky. As he looked up, he saw two unidentifiable silver objects, which he was able to film with a movie camera stored in his car. Although the processed film showed the silver flashes clearly, experts have yet to confirm exactly what Mariana saw.*

Defeat of a Fearsome Demon

Each year in late July or early August Nepalese villagers commemorate their triumph over Ghanta Karna, a towering demon who—despite the almost baby-faced innocence of the image at right—committed endless acts of slaughter and depravity that filled his mouth with blood. Answering the people's prayers for deliverance from this fiend, one of the Hindu gods transformed himself into a taunting frog, who teased Ghanta Karna into chasing him down a deep well. Spectators soon seized the opportunity to stone the trapped monster to death and then to burn the remains.

On Ghanta Karna day, children stationed at crossroads—traditional haunts of evil spirits—collect money from passersby for the creation of huge Ghanta Karna effigies that are later paraded around town and finally burned. Meanwhile, a man of the untouchable class takes on the persona of the demon and exacts pay of his own; to refuse him alms is to court disease or bad luck. When the costly revelries are over, the people go quickly to their homes. There they remain until dawn, lest the monster's ghost return to seek revenge.

A sworn enemy of the kindly Hindu creator god Vishnu, Ghanta Karna wears spherical bells for earrings so their tinkling will drown out any mention of Vishnu's name. He carries a club to bash his victims, and in the other hand is a flask, perhaps to collect their blood.

6 AUGUST

A good day for sea serpents. *Two well-known sightings of sea serpents occurred on this date in different years. In 1817, a large, snakelike monster was reportedly seen off Massachusetts near Gloucester harbor, where sightings occurred over the next two and a half weeks. Thirty-one years later, another serpent was reported to have passed close by the British naval frigate Daedalus on the same date.*

7 AUGUST

Death of a hero. *Once a year, the women of ancient Athens and Alexandria mourned the death of handsome Adonis, seen below dying of wounds inflicted by a boar—or so Greek myth said. During the festival of Adonia, women climbed ladders to the roofs of their houses, chanting, "Woe, woe Adonis." Folklorists believe Adonis and similar dying hero-gods represent the yearly growth and death of the crops; the women's tears, others say, may once have been considered sympathetic magic likely to bring rain.*

8 AUGUST

Dog days. *The "dog days" of summer—long hot spells that strike the middle latitudes around this time—derive their name from Sirius, the Dog Star, visible just before sunrise between July 3 and August 11. In ancient Egypt, the appearance of Sirius coincided with the rising of the fertile waters of the Nile and was cause for celebration. To the Greeks and Romans, however, Sirius marked only the heat and disease of summer, and their dog days were associated with irritability, ill health, and even death.*

9 AUGUST

Ghanta Karna Festival. *See above.*

An assistant helps the tightly swathed Burryman to a drink on a stop during his parade through the Scottish town of South Queensferry. Although the tradition doubtless harks back to an age-old magical belief, today it is simply an elaborate means of earning extra cash: The Burryman and his attendants spend the donated money at a town fair the next day.

10 AUGUST

A slip in time. *On this date in 1901 British teachers Anne Moberly (above) and Eleanor Jourdain (below) visited the French palace of Versailles and apparently stepped back in time. Among the long-dead figures they encountered were Queen Marie-Antoinette and the Comte de Vaudreuil, a courtier who once lured the thoughtless queen into permitting the performance of an antiroyalist play.*

11 AUGUST

Falling stars. *Since at least AD 830, sky watchers around the world have been amazed and delighted by the Perseid meteor shower, which like an astronomical Old Faithful appears every year at this time. Lighting up the night sky with as many as sixty flaming meteors an hour, the shower takes its name from the constellation Perseus, which marks the part of the sky where the shooting stars appear.*

12 AUGUST

A spirit reveals herself. *On this date in 1873, a London newspaper reported that Florence Cook, a British medium celebrated for her spirit summonings, had performed one of her most remarkable coups to date. Wearing a black dress and bound tightly to a chair, Cook was said to have caused her alleged spirit guide, Katie King, to appear in person during a séance. Skeptics noted that the ghost, though garbed in white, looked uncannily like Cook herself. However, they could not refute witnesses' assertions that Cook had remained confined to her chair throughout the event.*

13 AUGUST

Beginning of Mayan time. *Time was finite to the ancient Maya of Central America, who believed the universe itself commenced on this date in 3114 BC. According to ancient Mayan calculations, the cosmic progression of days will come to an end on December 23, AD 2012. On that day, says one astrological commentator who has seized on the Mayan prediction, human beings will be liberated from earthly bonds to begin a galactic—and cataclysmic—voyage.*

A Burr-Covered Scapegoat

On the second Friday of August in the Scottish coastal town of South Queensferry, the so-called Burryman (*left*) makes his annual appearance, matted from head to toe with thistle burrs. Wearing an outlandish hat made of seventy roses and a single dahlia, the Burryman walks slowly around the edge of the town, speaking to no one. Respectful townsfolk offer him donations, even though nobody seems to know the Burryman's purpose or remembers how he came into being.

Although the origins of South Queensferry's Burryman remain obscure, he is not unique; at one time there were a number of other Burrymen in fishing villages along the Scottish coast. One recent theory proposes that the figure represents a now-forgotten god of fertility, perhaps associated with the August fishing harvest. Another guess is that the Burryman evolved from a scapegoat figure meant to carry off communal guilt; people threw burrs that stuck on him, the theory goes, to relieve themselves of sin.

Festival for a New Age

During the mid-1980s, art historian José Argüelles came to the well-publicized conclusion that August 16, 1987, would be a very special day. The ancient Mayan and Aztec calendars, he said, foretold an alignment of celestial objects on that date that would bring about a five-year period of peace and spiritual cleansing in preparation for a twenty-first-century visit by otherworldly beings.

On the appointed day, hopeful New Age enthusiasts gathered at widely scattered "sacred sites" from Lake Titicaca in Bolivia to old ruins in New Mexico (*above*), ready and willing to be reborn. Some believed alien spaceships might appear or Jesus Christ might return. No sensational events occurred. In fact, even the planets were not aligned as some believed they would be. But the experience of traveling to distant spots and gathering with like thinkers proved satisfying for most participants, some of whom proclaimed the Harmonic Convergence the seminal experience of their lives.

14 AUGUST

Return of Scotland's Burryman. *See above.*

15 AUGUST

Ramadan. *Ramadan, the ninth month of Islam's lunar year, is by far the holiest. A time of repentance that may fall in any season, Ramadan observed by Muslims with an extraordinary fast: For the entire month, the faithful consume no scrap of food nor drop of water from sunrise to sunset, eating and drinking only after dark. With the rising of the next full moon, Ramadan comes to an end—a moment officially noted in some Islamic countries with cannon fire and also often celebrated with banquets. So festive is the post-Ramadan mood that Malaysian Muslims recommend this period as a time to patch up old quarrels.*

16 AUGUST

The Harmonic Convergence. *See above.*

17 AUGUST

Feast of Diana. *The Roman Feast of Diana honored the forest aspect of the ancient Roman goddess, seen below as a multiple-breasted mother figure, who according to one tradition mated with Rex Nemorensis, the King of the Wood, to let the earth bring forth fruit.*

18 AUGUST

Festival of Hungry Ghosts. *During the late summer, according to traditional Chinese belief, the spirits of the dead return to earth. Left untended and unfed, long-haired ghosts like those depicted above become angry, stealing food and bringing evil. During the Hungry Ghosts Festival—celebrated at about this time—villagers avert such ghostly antics by offering food, clothing, incense, models of houses and cars, and special currency like the two "hell bank notes" shown above. Each of the offerings is burned, since flames are thought to carry material objects into the spiritual realm.*

19 AUGUST

A farmyard visitor. *On this day in 1965, a sixteen-year-old boy in New York state was listening to the radio while milking the cows in his parents' barn. According to his story, static suddenly garbled the radio reception, and the motor on the milking machine abruptly quit. As a bull tied up in the barnyard let out an awful bellow, the boy rushed to the window to spy a fifty-foot-long, football-shaped object settling to the ground about a quarter mile away. The boy said it emitted a beeping sound and gave off a peculiar red vapor. Seconds later, it shot up to the clouds, where four other people claimed to have seen it.*

20 AUGUST

A laser disk for aliens. *Stored in a cover like the one shown below, an optical disk filled with whale songs, speeches by world leaders, and other sounds accompanied each of the crewless Voyager space probes, the first of which was launched from Cape Canaveral on this date in 1977. Although scientists believe that the chance of aliens stumbling across either probe is remote, mission planners did not want to miss any opportunity for contact with extraterrestrials.*

21 AUGUST

Sacrifice to Hercules. *On this day, ancient Romans made solemn sacrifice to muscular Hercules, the patron god of businessmen. All year long, merchants set aside a tenth of their profits for the god's benefit. When the very wealthy participated, such incredible banquets were held in the hero's honor that mountains of leftover delicacies had to be heaved into the river Tiber.*

22 AUGUST

Rosicrucian mystery. *On this date in 1623, Parisians awoke to find placards promoting a secret "Brotherhood of the Rosy Cross" posted all over the city. In the posters, members of the mysterious brotherhood—who quickly became known as Rosicrucians—offered "to bring our fellow men out of the error of death." Condemned by Church officials as satanic, the movement vanished from public view as quickly as it had appeared. Despite rumors of Rosicrucian activity in France, England, the Netherlands, and Germany, details remain disputed or altogether missing.*

23 AUGUST

The sun enters the sign of Virgo. *See below.*

24 AUGUST

A gory wedding night. *On this evening in 1669, young Janet Dalrymple was married to David Dunbar, heir to the Scottish estate of Baldoon, despite her own love for an impoverished suitor. According to legend, the wedding guests were horrified later that night by screams from the bridal chamber. Rushing to the scene, they found the bridegroom half-dead of several stab wounds and the bride completely insane; she died within the month, although her would-be victim recovered. Local tradition holds that Janet Dalrymple still haunts the ruins of Baldoon castle (above), plagued by the memories of a broken heart and a murderous rage.*

25 AUGUST

A wing-shaped UFO. *A man and woman in Albuquerque, New Mexico, were strolling on this night in 1951 when they observed a strange flying object. It was shaped like a wide inverted V with soft blue-green lights outlining its contours. Twenty minutes later, some three hundred miles to the east, a group of college professors in Lubbock, Texas, saw the same thing, and for the next two weeks there were dozens of sightings of the UFO in the vicinity of Lubbock. Some people claimed that the lights were merely reflections in the hazy sky, but many others were convinced that they were looking at the running lights of an alien spacecraft.*

Virgo: August 23-September 22

On August 23, the Sun enters Virgo, sign of the virgin. Astrologers say that the symbol refers not so much to chastity as it does to perfection, for Virgoans are unequivocal perfectionists.

Compulsively organized and meticulous, natives of Virgo strive to meet high standards using their fine-tuned and enormously practical minds. They love learning and have keen business sense, and their favorite task is to rescue order from the jaws of chaos. In the process, however, they sometimes become bogged down because of a tendency to pay too much attention to detail.

Virgoans are worriers. High-strung, they experience chronic bouts of anxiety and depression. They are often overly concerned with personal hygiene, which sometimes results in a host of psychosomatic ailments.

In their tidy and structured lives, Virgo natives find little time for romantic entanglements. They rarely tolerate the disarray of feelings that passion engenders, and any prospective mate must satisfy rigorous requirements in order to gain their approval.

Often, Virgoans prefer to remain alone, free to engage in pursuits they consider more worthwhile than sentimental dalliances. They are not homebodies, rejecting domesticity in favor of work with a great deal of mental stimulation. Virgoans shine as scientists, statisticians, gardeners, inspectors, craftsmen, secretaries, doctors, and nurses. Well-known Virgoans include German epic poet Goethe, former U.S. President Lyndon Johnson, and actress Raquel Welch.

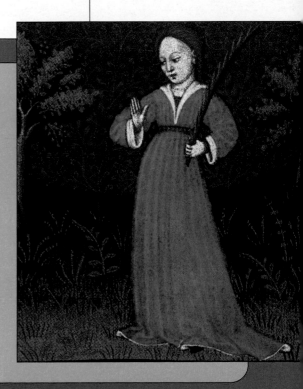

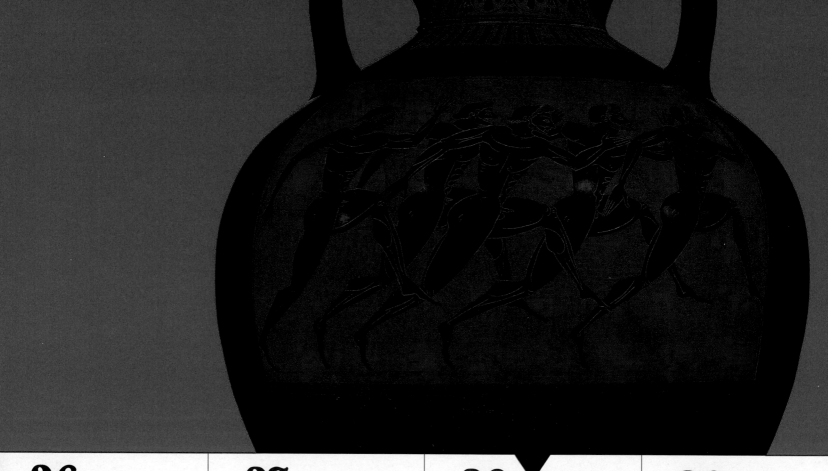

26 AUGUST

A god is born. *On this day, Hindu worshipers celebrate the periodic rebirth of Krishna, the blue-skinned eighth incarnation of the god Vishnu who is born again every time the world needs to be set right. Celebrants attend midnight services where a statue of the baby Krishna is hailed with cries of "Vijay!" or "Victory!" To welcome the infant deity, some worshipers then bathe a small image of Krishna and tuck him into a silver cradle.*

27 AUGUST

Worship at the Circus Maximus. *In late August, the ancient Romans held a festival in honor of Consus, god of the grain stores, which were replenished from the harvest at about this time. As sacrifices to Consus were made at an altar underneath the floor of the Circus Maximus, games in his honor were held in the stadium itself. Mules and horses were decked with garlands and given a day of rest, traditions that were later observed on the Christian feast of Saint Antony's Day.*

28 AUGUST

Origins of the Olympics. *World-class sporting events today, the Olympic Games once served a religious purpose as part of the late August harvest rituals of ancient Greece. Some have theorized the contests began as a race like the one depicted above, intended to choose the fittest champion to protect the spirit of the harvest during the hard winter months. Then as now, winners were hometown heroes. But due reverence had its limits: When one town erected a statue of its three-time boxing champion, jealous gods supposedly struck it down.*

29 AUGUST

Keeping witches calm. *At various times of the year, the Yoruba people of Nigeria celebrate Gelede, a rite meant to control old women past the age of childbearing. Traditionally considered witches, such women are thought to be subdued by the dances of men wearing masks like the one below.*

Bringing in the Ceremonial Sheaves

During the harvest season of August and September, agricultural societies often hold special rites to celebrate the beginning, or "first fruits," of the process as well as the final reaping. Lammas *(see August 1)* is a typical first-fruits ceremony for grain; another example is the Japanese practice of offering the first rice to the gods.

Because traditional agricultural societies had no guarantee that the growing season would return, the cutting of the last plant of the crop occasioned more anxiety than joy. Early Europeans believed that the spirit of the grain—the life force that would infuse next year's harvest—resided in the last stalk, which was often cut down by several reapers who shared the responsibility.

Once down, the stalk was in many cases fashioned into figures like the two shown here, known in the British Isles as corn dollies or kern babies. No child's toy, the corn dolly was a sacred talisman; its name may derive from the word *idol*. Often kept in a farmer's house until January, the dolly would then be plowed back into the field to work its magic on the next crop.

Folklore specialists believe that such corn dolly rituals may have descended from ceremonies in which real animal or human sacrifices were made to appease the great Corn Spirit. As late as the 1850s, the Khond people of Bengal, India, are said to have made human sacrifices to an Indian earth goddess, Tari Pennu. After a victim was dismembered and roasted, a shaman figure ate part of the charred flesh. The remains were then scattered over a plowed field, bringing future life out of sacrificial death.

30 AUGUST

Harvest-time rituals. *See above.*

31 AUGUST

A ghostly masquerade. *On this day in the Nigerian capital of Lagos, masqueraders called Eyos prowl the streets. These costumed demons are concealed in white robes and brandish long sticks; they are representatives of individual families and symbolize authority. People crossing the path of an Eyo must remove their hats and shoes as a sign of respect. If someone offends an Eyo, the demon will probably lash out with his stick. The Eyo's ritual walk was once thought to serve the purpose of cleansing the spirits of a family.*

The Power behind the Masks

Every spring, after dried maize seeds had been sown but before green shoots appeared, ancient Aztecs gathered for a festival called Tlacaxipeualiztli. Like most of their important ceremonies, this one centered on human sacrifice; but the process was particularly gruesome even by Aztec standards. A victim, usually a war prisoner, was taken to the temple, where the priests cut out his beating heart while he was still awake and struggling and offered it to Xipe Totec, god of springtime *(at right and below)*. That was just the beginning. Next they made deft cuts around his arms, legs, neck, and back and carefully skinned him. Then the warrior who had captured the prisoner donned the bloody skin and a mask made from the face and performed a dance beseeching the gods for new life. He wore the grisly garb for twenty days, till it rotted away from him. For the Aztecs, this ritual generated magic: Just as the warrior burst through the cracked skin of the dead victim, so would the maize plants imitate him and sprout through the golden shells of their seemingly dead seeds.

Although few approached the hideous grotesquery of these Aztec masks, since earliest times people have marked the progress of the year and sought to boost nature's bounty through seasonal masking rituals. A sampling of masks used in these festivals, some of which are still celebrated, appears on the following pages. Some masks supposedly enabled participants to tap the forces of the gods to encourage plentiful crops. Others were worn to honor spirits of certain animals so they would allow themselves to be caught. And some masks were thought to encourage general good fortune. They all served to channel cosmic power from the supernatural to earthly beings, ostensibly giving humans the means to control nature and to ensure their own survival.

This statuette and the greenstone mask at left both portray the Aztec deity Xipe Totec, also called the Flayed God, wearing skin stripped from a sacrificial victim. The mask was probably not meant to be worn, but like the statuette it does symbolize the violent spring ritual in which an Aztec warrior donned a mask of human skin.

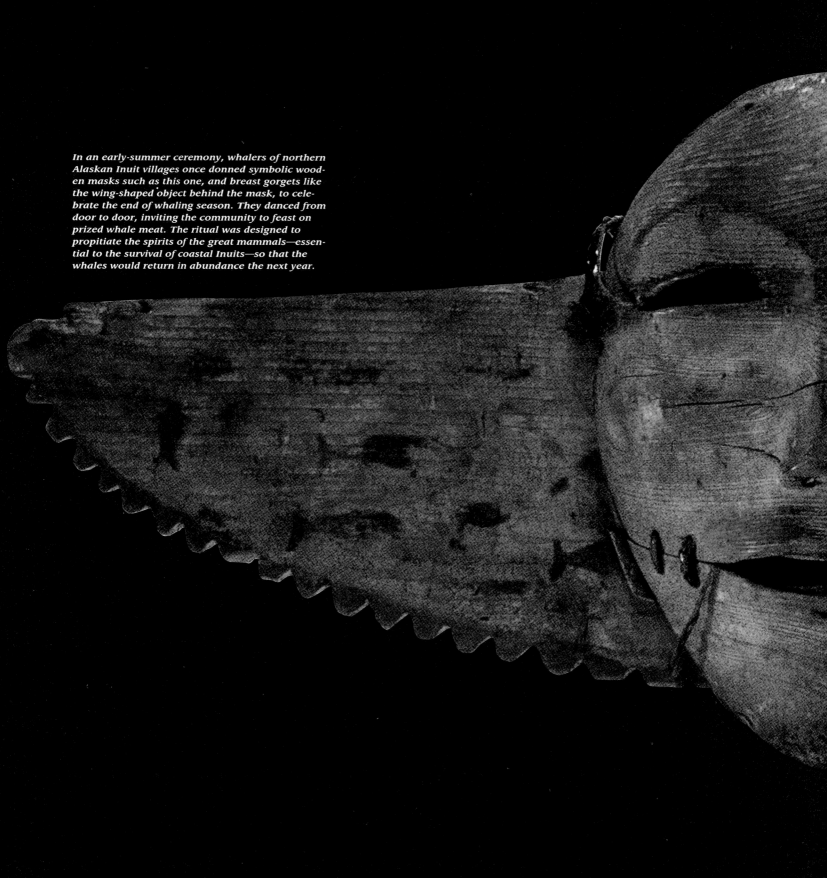

In an early-summer ceremony, whalers of northern Alaskan Inuit villages once donned symbolic wooden masks such as this one, and breast gorgets like the wing-shaped object behind the mask, to celebrate the end of whaling season. They danced from door to door, inviting the community to feast on prized whale meat. The ritual was designed to propitiate the spirits of the great mammals—essential to the survival of coastal Inuits—so that the whales would return in abundance the next year.

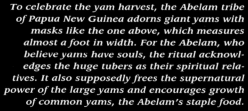

To celebrate the yam harvest, the Abelam tribe of Papua New Guinea adorns giant yams with masks like the one above, which measures almost a foot in width. For the Abelam, who believe yams have souls, the ritual acknowledges the huge tubers as their spiritual relatives. It also supposedly frees the supernatural power of the large yams and encourages growth of common yams, the Abelam's staple food.

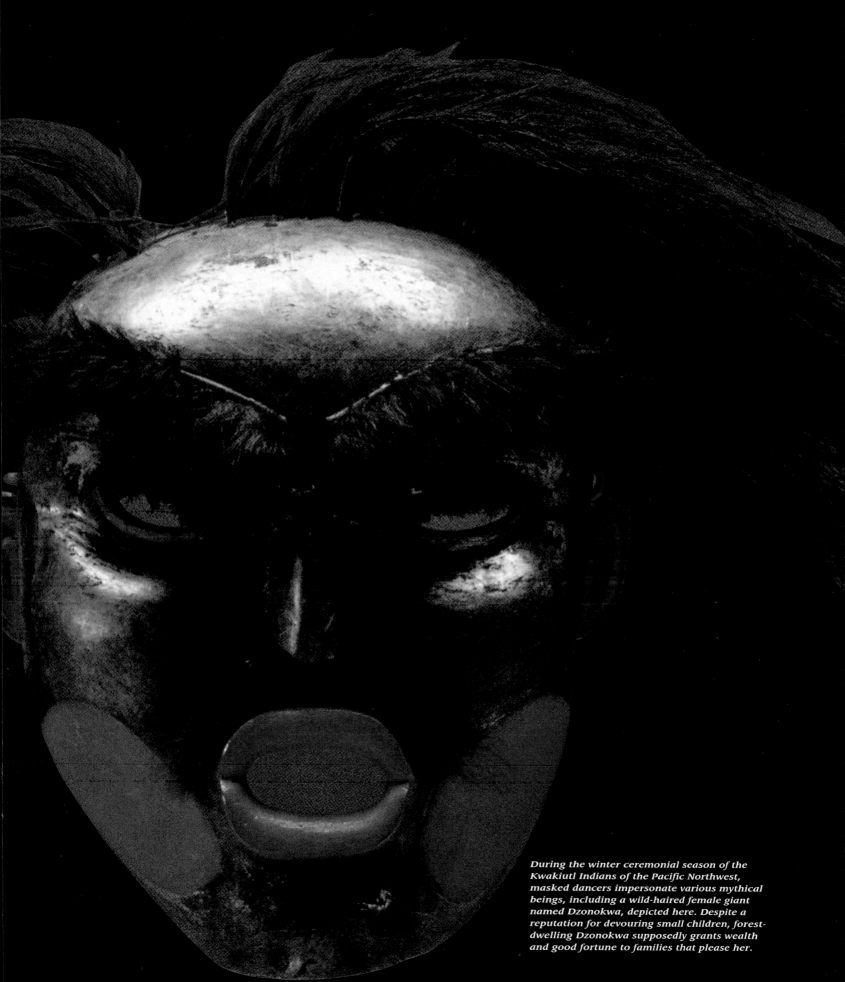

During the winter ceremonial season of the Kwakiutl Indians of the Pacific Northwest, masked dancers impersonate various mythical beings, including a wild-haired female giant named Dzonokwa, depicted here. Despite a reputation for devouring small children, forest-dwelling Dzonokwa supposedly grants wealth and good fortune to families that please her.

Dancers sporting cornhusk masks such as this one perform every year during the midwinter ceremony of New York's Seneca Indians. The masks symbolize the Husk Faces, a race of supernatural beings associated with the life-supporting crops of corn, beans, and squash. Their presence is believed to augur well for the coming growing season.

80

Fall

In autumn, as the growing cycle comes to an end and the shimmering heat of summer turns to eerie dusk, people around the world harvest their crops and store away the food that will see them through the winter. At once a season of plenty and the harbinger of deathly winter, autumn is marked by a wealth of rituals, beliefs, and uncanny occurrences, some of them chronicled in the pages that follow.

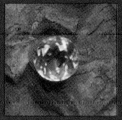

The sapphire is September's birthstone. The blue gem symbolizes truth, sincerity, justice, and constancy—and it was once believed to cure mental illness.

Many fall rites recognize both aspects of the season, celebrating its material abundance while also trying to preserve the harvest spirit through the approaching lean winter months. Until recently, European reapers ritually burned the last sheaf of wheat, suggesting the remnant of an earlier practice of animal or human sacrifice to the agricultural deities, while British farm hands teamed up to cut down the last stalk of corn together, so that no one person would bear the misfortune brought on by killing the Corn Spirit believed to live within it.

October's birthstone is the opal. The iridescent stone was once used in divination. If an opal was brilliant, it promised a project's success; if dull, it assured failure.

As the fall nights grow longer, people's thoughts turn naturally to unknown spirits of darkness—deities of the underworld, powerful ghosts of dead ancestors, and myriad other supernatural beings—including those half-humans who are believed subject to horrifying transformations, such as werewolves and vampires. Many old folk beliefs suggest that the normal protective barriers between our world and the next break down at this time of year, putting the living at risk. As a partial measure of protection, a number of autumn rites and ceremonies supposedly guard against dangerous, roving spirits of many kinds.

Ancient tales told that topaz, November's birthstone, rendered its wearer not only invisible but fireproof. The yellow jewel also helped win friends and lovers.

On Vampire Night in Rumania (see November 29), for example, custom calls for hanging garlic on doors and windows to keep the vampires from entering. Among the Celts, the dead themselves were thought to visit during Samhain, a festival which began at sunset on October 31. On this night, from which the modern holiday of Halloween descends, the Celts built huge bonfires on hilltops, wore masks and costumes to ward off footloose ghosts and demons, and put out offerings of food for the dead. No ritual, however, can prevent or even slow the approach of winter. As the sun itself dims and the days shorten further, autumn's one-time plenty is forgotten and the simple quest for survival replaces the eerie ambiguities of fall.

1 SEPTEMBER

Birth of Zoroaster. *A Persian prophet and mystic who lived in the sixth century BC, founder of the religion that bears his name, Zoroaster (left) was born on this day. Zoroastrianism teaches that the world is caught in a constant battle between good spirits, or ahuras, and evil spirits, known as daevas or divs. Zoroaster prophesied that the good would eventually triumph.*

Zoroaster, known by some as Zarathustra, writes in his study in this fifteenth-century Flemish painting. The prophet declared the existence of a single god, whom he called Ahura Mazda (or Ohrmazd), meaning wise lord.

The Rising Sun of Changing Woman

To mark the coming of age of a pubescent girl, Arizona's White Mountain Apache may celebrate a Sunrise or Coming Out Ceremony, often at this time of year. During the four-day-long rite, the young woman ritually becomes Changing Woman, a legendary Apache heroine who survived a great flood and magically gave birth to Son of Sun and Child of the Water. The girl's transformation

Kneeling upon a buckskin pad, a fourteen-year-old Apache girl dances during the Sunrise Ceremony that marks her passage into womanhood. Her godfather (far left) directs the dance with an eagle feather, and next to him, her father guards the sacred cane that will be hers for life.

into Changing Woman, the tribe members believe, not only ensures a long life for her; it also blesses everyone present.

For the Sunrise Ceremony, the girl dresses in a traditional buckskin blouse and ankle-length skirt. She wears one eagle-down feather on each shoulder, to help her through the rigorous dancing and running of the ceremony, and a third in her hair, to serve as guide and protector. She carries a specially decorated cane, a symbol of long life, which she will keep as long as she lives. Perhaps most important, she wears a disk of abalone shell on her forehead; as the rising sun's light strikes the shell on the first day of the ceremony, the power of Changing Wom-

an is believed to enter the young woman, to remain with her for life.

A godmother guides the girl through the ceremony of prayers, singing, dancing, storytelling, and feasting. The girl makes four circular runs, each wider than the one before, representing the four stages of life—childhood, adolescence, adulthood, and old age. Later, she lies face down on a deerhide rug so her body can be molded into the right shape for life by the godmother's massaging hands and feet. The girl's parents bless the pair by sprinkling pollen over them. When the ceremony is over, the young woman remains holy for four more days, receiving further instruction about life from her elders.

2 SEPTEMBER

Eleven lost days. *In 1751, the British Parliament abandoned the Julian calendar—then eleven days behind the solar year—and adopted the more accurate Gregorian calendar used on the Continent. The morning after Wednesday, September 2, 1751, Britons awoke to Thursday, September 14. Amid disputes over wages and rents, many people demanded their eleven days back. Some said that the Glastonbury Thorn, a tree noted for blooming on Christmas Day, repudiated the new calendar by flowering eleven days late.*

3 SEPTEMBER

The Exeter incident. *Early on September 3, 1965, two police officers and other witnesses reported a brightly lit, eighty-foot red sphere hovering near Exeter, New Hampshire. The sighting was never explained.*

Clear the path. *During Akwambo, the Path Clearing Festival, Ghana's Akan people symbolically clear a path to the village well. A priestess (below) then offers libations to the god of the well.*

4 SEPTEMBER

Apache Sunrise Ceremony. *See above.*

5 SEPTEMBER

Magnificent ruins. *On this date in 1871, German explorer Karl Mauch discovered Great Zimbabwe, the mysterious stone ruins of an ancient African fortress city in the country now called Zimbabwe.*

Ganesha Chaturthi. *This Hindu festival—the date of which changes on the Western calendar—honors Ganesh, the beneficent elephant-headed god of luck and prosperity. Worshipers parade decorated clay images of Ganesh to a river, a lake, or the sea and gently drown them (below). Then they take home soil from the water's edge, to ensure plenty.*

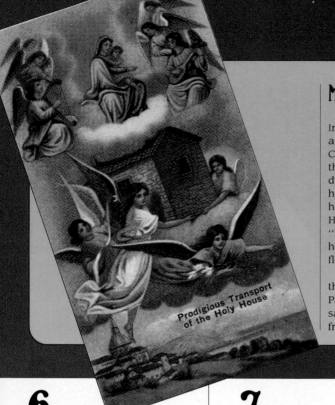

Prodigious Transport of the Holy House

Mary's Flying Cottage

In AD 326, the Roman Empress Helena made a pilgrimage to Palestine to celebrate the Christian conversion of her son, Constantine the Great. While she was there, she reputedly discovered the Holy House of Nazareth, home of Jesus, Mary, and Joseph, and the house in which the Virgin had been born. Helena recognized it, she said, by a certain "holy dread" it inspired in her. She had the house enveloped by a basilica, and pilgrims flocked to visit it.

Almost a thousand years later, in 1291, the armies of Islam were about to fall upon Palestine. In order to protect the Holy House, says Catholic tradition, angels descended from the heavens, picked up the small stone cottage, and carried it to a village in what later became Yugoslavia. But the angels grew concerned that the house was neglected there, and three years later they moved it again *(left)*, this time to the Italian town of Loreto on the other side of the Adriatic.

Regarding the appearance of the cottage as a miracle, the people of Loreto encircled the house with a wall and made it a holy shrine. It is also recorded that they sent a deputation of sixteen men to Nazareth whose mission was to find proof that the cottage came from there. They discovered that its dimensions matched the empty foundations where the Holy House had stood, and that an inscription there stated

6 SEPTEMBER

Their children's blood. *The Situa, an ancient Incan festival designed to ward off the deadly illnesses of the Southern Hemisphere's spring, got under way each September with the start of the rainy season. After a day of fasting, the Incas drew small amounts of their children's blood and mixed it with corn meal. They ate this paste, rubbed it on their bodies, and smeared it on their thresholds, to repel disease-bearing evil spirits. The festival culminated when the Inca, or emperor, wielding a feathered lance, sent four noble Incas running north, south, east, and west to rout the evil spirits from Incan lands.*

7 SEPTEMBER

Birth of Theosophy. *On this night in 1875, Madame Helena Petrovna Blavatsky and her salon of occultists agreed to form an organization for the study of arcane knowledge. The next day they formally founded the Theosophical Society. Henry Olcott, seen below with Blavatsky, was president, but Blavatsky was a prime mover in the Theosophical Society's work of spreading occult lore and ancient wisdom.*

8 SEPTEMBER

When angels transported the Holy House. *See above.*

9 SEPTEMBER

Chrysanthemum Day. *By an ancient Chinese custom, chrysanthemum wine is drunk on the ninth day of the ninth moon, to ensure long life. This is done in honor of T'ao Yuan-Ming, a Chinese poet who favored the chrysanthemum above all other flowers because it blooms alone in frosty autumn. After his death, the Chinese made him the god of the chrysanthemum. Ancient Japan set the same day aside as Choyo-no-Sekku, or Chrysanthemum Day, an important festival day on which the shogun received visits from his feudal lords. Modern Japanese celebrate Choyo-no-Sekku with competitive chrysanthemum shows.*

H. P. Blavatsky   H. S. Olcott

that the house had mysteriously vanished.

Around the cottage at Loreto, the Catholic Church later built a magnificent church of white marble. Over the centuries, thousands of pilgrims—including more than fifty popes—have visited the Holy House. Because Loreto possesses what it believes is the house in which Mary was born, the town's biggest festival occurs on September 8, the date observed as her birthday. Despite modern scholars' doubts about the truth of the Holy House tradition, the little cottage endures as a cherished shrine. At its door, a plaque proclaims, "Let those who are impure tremble to enter into this sanctuary. The whole world has no place more sacred."

10 SEPTEMBER

Horn Dance. *See below.*

11 SEPTEMBER

Celebrating a pardon. *For three days starting on September 11, members of the Nichiren sect of Japanese Buddhism pay homage to their founder, Nichiren. This outspoken thirteenth-century priest so angered government authorities that he was arrested and sentenced to beheading. But when lightning struck near the execution site, officials reduced the sentence to exile on a nearby island. Freed from exile on September 12, 1271, Nichiren spent the rest of his life teaching his distinct form of Buddhism. At his annual festival, Nichiren's modern-day followers shout prayers while beating fan-shaped drums.*

12 SEPTEMBER

A pumpkin king. *Every year at about this time, Parisians used to gather at the central market for a curious ritual. La Fête du Roi Potiron—or King Pumpkin's Day—featured a giant pumpkin fitted out with a paper-and-tinsel crown. Revelers carried the overgrown vegetable through the market on a throne, while vendors jokingly paid their respects. Then, without further ado, everyone set about carving the pumpkin for use in a traditional soup. This observance may have harked back to ancient customs of crop propitiation.*

13 SEPTEMBER

Egyptian All-Souls' Day. *The ancient Egyptian goddess Nepthys, or Nebthet (above), whose headdress is made up of the two hieroglyphs of her name—a basket (neb) placed on the sign for a palace (het)—is a protectress of the dead. On this day, fires were lit in her honor.*

Ancient Reindeer Ghosts

There is no other dance like it in all the folkways of Europe. It begins at the crack of dawn each year on the Monday after Wakes Sunday, the first Sunday after September 4, as the costumed dancers gather outside the village church at Abbots Bromley in Staffordshire, England. All male, they include a fool, Robin Hood riding a hobbyhorse, a man dressed as Maid Marian, a bowman, two musicians, and six deer—men wearing heavy wooden replicas of reindeer antlers.

Throughout the day the group wends its way through the village and neighboring countryside, stopping at intervals to perform the Horn Dance for waiting crowds. Toward evening, the men return to the village center for one last dance, then return the antlers to the church until the following year.

The fact that reindeer have been extinct in Britain for a thousand years suggests that the Horn Dance was a festival of ancient, pagan times and was perhaps intended to ensure fertility or good hunting.

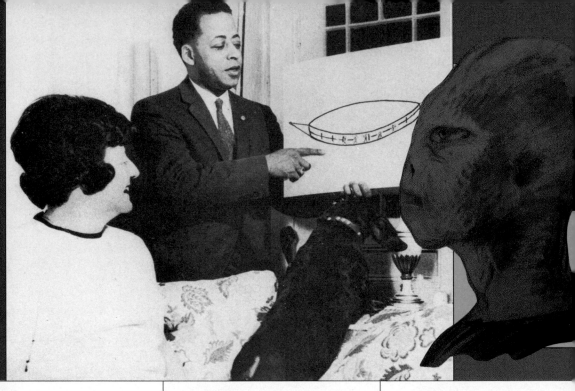

Barney Hill displays a sketch he made of the UFO he and his wife (seated) said they encountered in 1961. He points out a double row of windows through which, he said, he first saw the unearthly beings. The drawing at right of an alien with broad eyes and slitlike nose was based on a description the Hills gave under hypnosis.

14 SEPTEMBER

Saint Francis receives stigmata. *Early on this day in 1224, Francis of Assisi had a vision of a six-winged seraph carrying an image of Jesus on the cross. Immediately the monk found in his own hands, feet, and side the five wounds of the crucified Christ—stigmata he is said to have borne the rest of his life.*

Holy Cross Day. *On this date in AD 312, just before a battle, the Roman emperor Constantine I reportedly saw in the sky a cross inscribed "In hoc signo vinces"—"By this sign you will conquer." Commemorating his vision and the victory he won that day, Constantine instituted the Feast of the Holy Cross.*

15 SEPTEMBER

The Star of Bethlehem. *As the sun set in the west on this date in the year 7 BC, an unusually bright body rose in the east. This brilliant "star" was formed by the rare conjunction of Saturn and Jupiter, the planet of kings, in the constellation Pisces—the Fishes. This fact has led some astrologers to suggest that September 15 is the true birth date of Christ and that the Jupiter-Saturn conjunction was the Star of Bethlehem observed in the east by the three wise men, or Magi.*

16 SEPTEMBER

Megaliths explained. *Today is the feast of the Breton Saint Cornély who is thought to have created the Carnac megaliths by turning hostile soldiers to stone. Cornély is also patron of horned animals; on this day Brettons lead oxen through his shrine at midnight for blessing. Priests turn a blind eye to the huge beasts lumbering through the church.*

17 SEPTEMBER

The Eleusinia. *This ancient Greek festival, renowned for its secret rites, or mysteries, honored Demeter, goddess of agriculture. Tradition relates that Demeter taught the secrets of growing crops to the Eleusinians for their kindness when her daughter, Persephone, was abducted by Hades, lord of the underworld.*

Lighting the way with torches, Persephone (right) returns from the underworld to her mother, Demeter, in this fifth-century-BC bas-relief. Demeter holds in one hand the staff she used in her search for her daughter. In her other hand she carries sheaves of wheat, symbolizing her gift of thanksgiving upon Persephone's return.

Lost Hours on a Lonely Road

On the night of September 19, 1961, Betty and Barney Hill (*far left*) were headed home to Portsmouth, New Hampshire, from a Canadian vacation. They later related that while driving on U.S. Route 3, they saw a bright starlike object moving across the southwestern sky. Barney pulled off the road several times to let Betty study the object through binoculars. They decided it was some kind of unusual airplane.

Suddenly, the Hills' account went on, the large, disk-shaped craft flew toward the couple's parked car, stopping just above the deserted road in front of them. Barney took the binoculars and got out of the car for a closer look. He was astonished to see, behind the portholes of the hovering craft, five to eleven humanlike figures moving about. "I don't believe it! I don't believe it! This is ridiculous!" he yelled to Betty.

Barney ran back to the car and the Hills sped home—or so they thought. But at home, the pair found they had "lost" more than two hours' time between their encounter with the UFO and their return home. What had happened during those hours?

The Hills had no answer to that question until several years later, when they consulted a prominent Boston psychiatrist about Barney's nervousness and insomnia and Betty's nightmares—problems that had begun after the Hills saw the UFO. Under hypnosis, each spouse recounted a terrifying and incredible tale: On that lonely road in September of 1961, they had been taken into the strange spacecraft and subjected to a sometimes painful physical examination by beings from another world.

Although skeptics consider the Hills' story pure fabrication, similar tales of alien abduction have surfaced around the globe, leading some UFO investigators to hypothesize that the creatures may be conducting genetic studies of humans, perhaps to create a human-alien hybrid.

18 SEPTEMBER

Paying heed to an earthwork. *Each year for two gala days in September, Britons flock to the site of the Uffington White Horse—a colossal figure of a galloping steed cut into the pale clay of a Berkshire hillside. They come to take part in a centuries-old tradition called Scouring the White Horse. The principal objective of the gathering is to eliminate the weeds that would otherwise obliterate the horse's silhouette. But when the chores are completed, participants stay on hand for a festival of games and athletic competition.*

19 SEPTEMBER

A couple's story of a strange encounter. *See above.*

20 SEPTEMBER

Solar birthday. *Living south of the equator, Incas marked the spring equinox on or near this day. They waited silently in the dark at a mountaintop temple for the golden rays of the sun, their god, to flash over the peak. Great rejoicing and feasts, animal sacrifice, and divination occupied the rest of the day.*

21 SEPTEMBER

A day of divination. *In some countries, people seek to predict the future on this, Saint Matthew's Day. An old adage avers, for instance, that if the weather is fair today, it shall continue to be so for four weeks. And German girls once made fortune-telling wreaths on this day. Some were straw, some evergreen. In the dark, each girl chose one: Green meant a happy marriage and good health, while brown foretold sickness and unhappiness.*

Libra: September 23-October 22

The period of the astrological year known as Libra begins September 23. Because it occurs near the autumnal equinox, when day is equal to night, Libra is symbolized by the Scales, representing balance and harmony.

Libra is associated with Venus, the planet named for the Roman goddess of beauty. According to astrologers, people born during Libra desire beauty in all aspects of life, particularly in their social interactions. Human relationships are paramount for Librans, who cultivate each new friendship with care and respect. They toil indefatigably to make people feel comfortable and happy, affirming their own sense of self-worth by reaching out to others.

They also battle for social justice, as their scale symbol suggests, using grace and charm to exact compromises from opponents. But because they become so emotionally involved in the lives of others, they may appear meddlesome and judgmental. They mean well, but they are unable to keep their distance—for fear of being alone.

As a result, Librans are so extroverted that they do not know themselves particular-

22 SEPTEMBER

The onset of autumn. *Astronomically, fall commences around September 22 on a day that has exactly twelve hours of daylight and twelve of darkness and is known as the equinox, from the Latin for "equal night." Some cultures called this day the Witches' Thanksgiving; ancient Celts called it Mabon, to honor Queen Mab of the fairy people. In Japan, the autumnal equinox is a holiday called Higan, meaning "other shore," or heaven. On this day, the sun sets due west, where Buddhists believe heaven lies. To honor the dead, Buddhists visit cemeteries and pray for the souls of departed ancestors.*

23 SEPTEMBER

The sun enters the sign of Libra. *See above.*

24 SEPTEMBER

An annual rebirth. *In autumn, ancient Egyptians marked the approach of planting season by commemorating the death and rebirth of the god Osiris (below) with music, dancing, and ceremonial plantings.*

25 SEPTEMBER

Happy days for Durga. *For roughly two weeks in this period of the year, at a time determined astronomically, the people of India celebrate Durga Puja in honor of the ten-armed goddess Durga, the Divine Mother of the Universe. In Indian tradition, Durga conquered the thousand-headed king of demons, Mahisasura. The festival is a time of joy, when children express their respect for their parents, and adults settle quarrels with friends and neighbors. At Durga Puja, many families hold their annual reunions and celebrate family life.*

ly well. They neglect to give adequate consideration to their own thoughts and needs, bending instead to the influence of others. And when forced to make an independent choice, natives of this sign frequently succumb to indecision and vacillation.

Famous Librans include actress Angela Lansbury, television host Johnny Carson, singer Bruce Springsteen, and former president Jimmy Carter—whose Libran diplomacy and pacifism facilitated the 1978 summit meeting that led to a peace treaty between Egypt and Israel.

26 SEPTEMBER

Glorifying God and apples. *The real Johnny Appleseed—John Chapman—was born on this day in 1774. As a young man, Chapman suffered a blow to the head that resulted in what he believed to be a vision of heaven. God's home, he reported, was distinguished by an abundance of blooming apple trees. Following this epiphany, Chapman made it his mission to plant apples and preach the Christian scripture. He wandered the American prairies sowing seeds and reading from the Bible. In the process, he earned a place in American folklore.*

27 SEPTEMBER

The Moon Festival. *See below.*

28 SEPTEMBER

Birth of Confucius. *The great Chinese philosopher and moral teacher Confucius (above) is believed by some to have been born on this date in 551 BC.*

Yom Kippur. *This solemn day of rest, prayer, fasting, and ritual purification ends the Ten Days of Penitence that begin with the Jewish New Year, Rosh Hashanah. And like that holiday, Yom Kippur occurs on movable dates determined by moon phases. In ancient times, a scapegoat, a symbolic sin bearer, was turned out into the desert to carry away the sins of the people.*

29 SEPTEMBER

Michaelmas, or Saint Michael's Day. *Many customs are associated with Michaelmas, the day Christians set aside to honor Saint Michael, chief of the archangels who chased the devil Lucifer from heaven. In England, for example, people used to refuse to pick blackberries after this date, believing that the devil, who had landed on a prickly blackberry bush when he fell from heaven, cursed the berries and spit or urinated on them each autumn on Michaelmas. On the Scottish island of Saint Kilda, families still bake and eat a special cake on this day to ensure Saint Michael's protection in the coming year.*

Ladies' Treats for the Hare in the Moon

One of the most joyous events of the Chinese year, the Moon Festival, or Chung-Ch'iu, falls on the full moon of the eighth month of the Chinese lunar calendar—the autumn harvest moon. As the climax of the growing season, the Moon Festival is a time to give thanks for a bountiful harvest.

Because the moon in Chinese thought symbolizes the female principle of yin, the rites are carried out by the women of each family. In their courtyards, they arrange a special altar on which they place a picture and sometimes a small figure of the Moon Hare, a creature that, in Chinese mythology, inhabits the moon. When moonlight fills the courtyard, the ceremony begins. The women set offerings on the altar—five platters of different kinds of fruit and thirteen "mooncakes," small, spicy, circular cakes to represent the thirteen months of the lunar year. Some offer beans, said to be a favorite of the Moon Hare. The women light incense and, one by one, approach the altar and bow. Then the picture of the Moon Hare is burned to free its soul to return to the moon.

Goal of a Sacred Journey

According to one classical formulation, the faith of Islam requires of its followers five things: belief, prayer, charity, fasting, and pilgrimage. To fulfill the last requirement, every Muslim must make at least one pilgrimage to Mecca, where the prophet Muhammad was born. According to the Koran,

In this 1901 photograph, Muslim pilgrims stand barefoot around the cloth-draped shrine called the Ka'ba in the holy city of Mecca. Most pilgrims wear only two simple white sheets, as a reminder that all are equal before God.

30 SEPTEMBER

A star's life after death. *On this date in 1955, James Dean died at the age of twenty-four in a car crash, but the handsome, brooding actor lives on as a supernatural cult hero. Some thirty thousand fans gather each year in Fairmount, Indiana, where Dean grew up and is buried, to mark the anniversary of his death. Many believe he speaks to them. One says he told her through her Ouija to go to a certain road, then briefly appeared there "in his East of Eden outfit." Another heard Dean's booted feet "walking back to his grave." Police shooed away eight academics holding a séance on the grave. But Fairmount likes the visitors' money and has made the anniversary a three-day festival.*

1 OCTOBER

Pilgrimage to Mecca. *See above.*

2 OCTOBER

Thanks to the angels. *In 1672, Pope Clement X proclaimed this date Guardian Angels Day, an occasion for people to give special thanks to the angels like the one below and for the protection such celestial guardians provide.*

3 OCTOBER

Reunion with the gods. *At about this time, the Cherokee nation once celebrated its Cementation and Propitiation Festival, in which men exchanged the clothes they were wearing to symbolize human union with Cherokee deities. Celebrants later immersed themselves in running water to wash away unseen barriers to the gods.*

Islam's holy book, this pilgrimage, or hajj, must be timed so the pilgrim is in Mecca on the seventh day of the month of Dhu'l-hijjah—a date that varies from year to year on Western calendars. Once a Muslim has completed the hajj, he or she may assume the title Hajji, pilgrim, a mark of high honor.

Before reaching Mecca—a city still forbidden to non-Muslims—the pilgrims must bathe, pray, and don special garments. When they enter the city, they head straight for the Ka'ba, the veiled shrine at left. Said to have been built by Abraham and his son Ishmael, from whom the Arab people descended, the Ka'ba has been gradually repaired until only one of its building blocks—the Black Stone,

in its eastern corner—is believed to date from Abraham's day. Each pilgrim walks around the Ka'ba seven times, striving to touch or kiss the Black Stone, as did the prophet Muhammad when he rededicated it to the service of the one god, Allah.

After paying their respects to the Ka'ba, pilgrims pass on to the small domed Mosque of Abraham and drink from the sacred Well of Ishmael nearby. According to tradition, this well sprang miraculously from the sand to save Ishmael and his mother when both were abandoned in the desert.

Pilgrims then climb the holy hills of Safa and Marwa, journeying between them seven times and stopping only to recite prayers. On

the eighth day of Dhu'l-hijjah comes the so-called standing, in which hundreds of thousands of worshipers gather on the nearby Plains of Arafat to stand and pray from noon to sunset. After nightfall, each pilgrim collects seventy pebbles from the desert. The stones are later thrown at three ancient pillars that represent the evils of the world. A final animal sacrifice ends the hajj.

Some pious travelers, however, go on to the city of Medina, where Muhammad fled when Mecca disowned him, to pray in the Mosque of the Prophet. Muhammad wrote that one prayer recited in this mosque has more effect than a thousand prayers said in any location other than the Ka'ba in Mecca.

4 OCTOBER

An ancient harvest rite. *During the Jewish harvest festival of Sukkoth, which takes place at about this time, worshipers eat their meals in outdoor booths, built from tree boughs. A time of renewal and thanksgiving, Sukkoth also includes a special prayer for rain.*

5 OCTOBER

Dances with the corn goddess. *In Lithuania, the reaping of the last sheaf of grain at about this time is marked by the Nubaigai celebration. On some farms, workers dress the last sheaf—called the Old Woman—in women's clothes and dance with it for good luck. Nubaigai often ends as a full-blown festival, with food and drink, dancing, and games.*

6 OCTOBER

A god wakes up after a long nap. *See below.*

7 OCTOBER

A hybrid religious festival. *On this day, fifteenth-century German peasants launched Kermesse, a week-long holiday that blended Christianity and paganism. First, they visited a remote spot where the year before they had buried a sacred symbol— sometimes a Christian icon, sometimes a pagan one. Digging it up, they mounted it atop a gaily decorated pole and marched it to town. Days of games, feasting, dancing, irreverent hymn singing, and other antics followed. At week's end, the townsfolk donned mourning garb and returned the Kermesse symbol to the earth for another year.*

Vishnu's Bed of Snakes

Each autumn in Nepal, Hindu worshipers of the great god Vishnu hold a nine-day religious festival honoring their transcendant protector and redeemer. The celebration, one of the most auspicious of the Hindu year, includes Haribodhini Ekadasi—the day, in Hindu tradition, when Vishnu wakes from his annual four-month rest on a subterranean bed of snakes, a scene vividly depicted in the seventh-century statuary at left.

To mark the god's awakening, the faithful bathe in sacred waters, chant Vishnu's name 1,008 times, and make secret—and thus more truly charitable—offerings of alms by hiding them in unripe pumpkins. Should Vishnu's worshipers fail to honor him at this time, tradition holds, they risk rebirth as crowing roosters or human mutes.

8 OCTOBER

A high road to escape from mysterious death. *See below.*

9 OCTOBER

Aliens in the Soviet Union. *On this day in 1989, the Soviet news agency Tass reported that a banana-shaped UFO carrying giant "humanlike" aliens and a tiny robot had landed in the city of Voronezh. The strange beings allegedly took a walk, then boarded their craft again and disappeared into space.*

10 OCTOBER

A ritual parade. *The two-week Festival of Light held in mid-October in the Brazilian city of Belém includes a penitential parade of tens of thousands of worshipers, many of whom go barefoot and carry heavy weights for their sins.*

11 OCTOBER

An alien abduction. *On this date in 1973, Calvin Parker and Charles Hickson were by their own account abducted from Pascagoula, Mississippi, and taken aboard what was apparently a spaceship. There they later claimed to have been examined by eyeless, gray-skinned creatures, one of which is depicted at left in a sketch based on their description.*

Climbing above It All

Midway through autumn, the Chinese celebrate Chung Yeung, the Festival of High Places—a holiday that commemorates the legendary scholar Huan Ching. According to tradition, Huan Ching, who is said to have lived in the village of Joo-an more than 2,000 years ago, was warned by a soothsayer to take his family up into the hills on this day to avoid a disaster that would devastate the village below. After passing on the warning to others, Huan Ching and his family fled into the hills. When the refugees returned, they found that every living creature left behind had mysteriously died.

In modern times, families recall that escape on Chung Yeung Day by flying kites from local hills or mountains, as in the scene at left. The kites, which are thought to carry away impending evils, often take the form of such good omens as bats, fish, and butterflies. The traditional accompanying picnic includes chrysanthemum wine, which Huan Ching supposedly took with him when he fled, and special cakes that are said to bring good luck and career advancement when eaten in high places.

12 OCTOBER

The wickedest man. *The notorious British occultist Aleister Crowley (above), the so-called wickedest man in the world, was born on this date in 1875. A member of several secret sects and founder of one called the Silver Star, or Argentinum Astrum, Crowley roamed the world preaching his own form of "magick," based on sex and drugs. (He added the "k" to distinguish his occult ceremonies from stage magic.) Crowley, who summed up his philosophy in four words, "Do what thou wilt," was plagued by scandal throughout his adult life and died bankrupt in 1947.*

13 OCTOBER

Great wonders in Portugal. *See below.*

14 OCTOBER

Intragalactic fraternity. *Today is Interplanetary Confederation Day, sponsored by the UFO-enthusiast Unarius Foundation. The purpose of the event is to recognize the other planets with which Earth shares the Milky Way galaxy.*

15 OCTOBER

Cat-and-mouse with a UFO. *While flying over Japan on this date in 1948, the crew of a U.S. Air Force F-61 Black Widow night fighter picked up a mysterious aircraft on radar. The unidentified craft was flying at about two hundred miles per hour, but each time the Black Widow attempted to close in on it, the intruder accelerated abruptly, reaching speeds of perhaps twelve hundred mph. Then the strange craft would slow down again, as if challenging the jet to give chase. On one pass, the crew reported seeing the silhouette of a "rifle bullet," twenty to thirty feet long. The frustrated crew could gather no other information.*

The Miracles at Fátima

On May 13, 1917, three Portuguese children tending sheep near the town of Fátima saw a beautiful woman they identified as the Virgin Mary. Veiled in a white cloth bordered in gold, the mysterious figure told ten-year-old Lucia dos Santos, nine-year-old Francisco Marto, and seven-year-old Jacinta Marto that she would return to meet them on the thirteenth day of each of the next five months.

Fifty villagers accompanied the children on June 13, the first appointed date, but the adults heard only whispering noises as Mary supposedly appeared. The crowd grew to 5,000 on July 13, when Lucia said the Virgin told her to pray for peace. Prevented by the government from returning on August 13, the children came back on September 13 with a crowd of 30,000—some of whom saw falling flower petals that vanished in midair.

On October 13, a full 70,000 pilgrims—some of them shown here with Jacinta—turned out for the Virgin's final visit, when all present observed a huge silver disk in

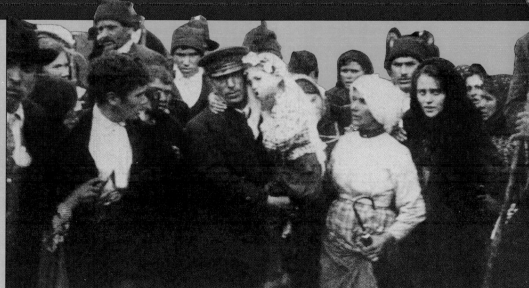

the sky. Spinning and throwing off colored flames, the disk dived toward the crowd only to stop and soar away.

Nor was that the end of the Fátima story. During her visits, the Virgin Mary had apparently shared a number of predictions with the children, including a forecast that the future Soviet Union would cause great trouble but would later be converted to Catholicism. Some believe that prophecy began to come true in August 1991 as the Communist party lost power after a failed Soviet coup.

16 OCTOBER

A providential escape. On this night one year in the late 1640s, British trader Sir John Gayer found himself alone in the Arabian desert, confronted by a savage lion. Recalling the biblical story of Daniel, who was miraculously preserved after being thrown into a den of lions, Sir John prayed fervently for similar protection, and the lion stalked away. Back in England, the grateful knight established a fund at London's Church of Saint Katherine Cree to pay for an annual sermon about his escape. The "Lion's Sermon" has been preached on or about the anniversary of Gayer's ordeal ever since.

17 OCTOBER

Food for the gods. On this date falls the Japanese Shinto ceremony known as the Kanname-Sai, or God-Tasting Event, in which the first fruits of the year's rice crop are offered to the sun goddess and other imperial ancestors.

18 OCTOBER

Thesmophoria. During this ancient Greek festival held during mid-October, women retrieved pig carcasses from snake-filled chasms into which the dead swine had earlier been thrown. Mixing the rotten flesh with seed, the women prayed to the grain goddess Demeter for abundant crops.

19 OCTOBER

Sticky pickles and a god of luck. A popular event in Tokyo is the annual fair known as Bettara-Ichi, held on this date near the shrine of Ebisu, one of the seven Shinto gods of luck. Streets near the shrine are lined with stalls where people buy good luck pieces and religious images, but the favorite items are sticky pickled radishes called bettara that are sold tied to straw ropes. Mischievous youngsters traditionally run among the fairgoers, swinging the pickles at their friends and shouting "bettara, bettara"—sticky, sticky—in playful warning.

Scorpio: October 23-November 21

The season of Scorpio begins on October 23. Long considered the darkest and most treacherous sign of the zodiac, Scorpio is ruled by Mars—god of war—and Pluto, god of the underworld.

Those born under this sign are said to have the tendency to be resentful, inflexible, secretive, and prone to jealous obsessions. They experience virtually uncontrollable unconscious urges. Their more positive attributes, say astrologers, include a gifted imagination, a strong sense of purpose, and an ability to see projects through. Newscaster Dan Rather and Charles, Prince of Wales—both natives of the sign—could be said to demonstrate this kind of Scorpio grit.

Scorpio's three symbols shed light on this complex sign. The first, the scorpion, represents Scorpios' capacity for cruelty. The eagle, on the other hand, with its keen vision, symbolizes Scorpios' trenchant perceptiveness. And the phoenix—sacrificed to flames then reborn from them—reveals their survival instinct: Although their troubles may consume them, Scorpios eventually rise triumphant from the pyre.

Astrologers say the sign of Scorpio rules the genitals, and those born during its season experience their sexuality intensely. For some Scorpio natives, sex is sheer eroticism—to be strictly denied or heartily embraced. For others, intercourse verges upon spiritual enlightenment.

20 OCTOBER

Bigfoot filmed. *On this date in 1967, former rodeo rider Roger Patterson reportedly spotted a huge, apelike figure in the wooded highlands of northern California. Believing it to be the legendary humanoid creature called Bigfoot, Patterson reached for his home-movie camera. The resulting twenty-four feet of film is considered the best evidence yet that Bigfoot does exist.*

21 OCTOBER

A tragic premonition. *On October 21, 1966, half a million tons of coal waste slid onto a school and other buildings in Aberfan, Wales (below, left), killing 140 people. One victim, nine-year-old Eryl Mai Jones (below), had apparently foreseen her fate. The previous morning, Eryl told her mother she had dreamed the school could not be found, because "something black had come down all over it."*

22 OCTOBER

Purifying fires. *Japan's Hi Matsuri, or Fire Festival, is celebrated this night in the village of Kurama, near Kyoto. Through streets ablaze with bonfires, people carry flaming torches like those below in a frenzied procession of fire, considered a purifying element. The brilliant parade ends at a shrine where at midnight, it is said, the gods descend to earth.*

23 OCTOBER

Swallows leave Capistrano. *Since 1798, swallows have flown south at this time from nests near the former site of California's San Juan Capistrano mission, destroyed by an earthquake in 1812. Local tradition holds that the birds come and go with remarkable regularity, leaving on this date—Saint John's Day—and returning on Saint Joseph's Day, March 19. Capistrano has recently become too crowded for the birds, who have moved on to a hospital six miles away.*

Halloween's Old, Dark Roots

Across northern Europe and the British Isles, the ancient Celts once celebrated Samhain, or "summer's end," on the last night of October. After bringing in their cattle from pasture to spend the winter under shelter, the Celtic people held a great fire festival to mark the beginning of winter and to remember the dead. On this night, which was also their New Year's Eve, the Celts believed that the spirits of dead loved ones might return to warm themselves by the hearth; families left their doors unlocked and set out food and drink for their otherworldly guests.

Witches, hobgoblins, and other malevolent beings were also expected to be at large, and people danced around bonfires kindled to keep evil spirits at bay—and to encourage the dimming sun not to go out entirely. But if Samhain was a night of spiritual apprehension and danger, it also offered glimpses into the future. Myriad methods of divination, purporting to reveal who would marry, who would prosper, and who would die in the coming year, were considered effective only on this fateful evening.

In the ninth century, the Church Christian-

24 OCTOBER

A time of blind faith. *In Germany, the third Sunday in October is Kirmes, a holiday that evolved from the Renaissance Kermesse festival (October 7). Chiefly a church festival today, Kirmes was once a turning point in the agricultural year. With the fall harvest complete and the seeds for the winter crops sown, the farmers were, for a short time, purely at the mercy of nature. They could do nothing more to prepare for the future except put their faith in a higher power. At Kirmes, they gave thanks for the old year's bounty while praying for good fortune in the new.*

25 OCTOBER

The shoemaker saints. *In the third century, Christian brothers named Crispin and Crispinian traveled from Rome to the French town of Soissons to work as cobblers and to preach the Gospel. Legend has it that angels helped the brothers make shoes for the poor by delivering leather to their shop at night. Arrested and sentenced to death for their beliefs, the pious brothers coolly survived four execution attempts before consenting to be beheaded. The Roman Catholic church later canonized the brother martyrs as the patron saints of shoemakers and set aside this date as their feast day.*

26 OCTOBER

Let there be earth. *According to the calculations of seventeenth-century Anglican archbishop James Ussher, chronological references throughout the Bible imply that God created the earth on October 26, 4004 BC.*

27 OCTOBER

Eating magical apples. *By tradition, unmarried men and women in Cornwall purchase brightly polished apples known as Allan Apples on this day and sleep with them under their pillows. Before dawn, each must wake up and eat the fruit soundlessly, then go outside and sit under a tree. The first person to pass by is thought to be the apple eater's future spouse.*

ized the old Celtic New Year by proclaiming it All Hallows' or All Saints' Day *(see November 1)*. The previous day, October 31, thus became known on the calendar of Christian festivals as All Hallows' Eve, or Halloween. Despite the change in nomenclature, however, many old Samhain customs were still observed on this date.

Well into the late 1800s, in parts of Wales and Scotland, families continued to gather around bonfires on All Hallows' Eve for a ceremony in which each person threw a marked white stone into the flames. If any stone could not be found among the ashes the next day, it was feared that its thrower would die during the coming year. Young people bobbed for apples afloat in tubs of water; if a maiden caught one, she would sleep with it under her pillow in hopes of dreaming of her future husband.

To frighten away evil spirits, countryfolk in Ireland, Scotland, and the north of England dressed in robes and masks, a custom known as guising, before venturing out of doors. Irish guisers often trooped from farm to farm demanding edible tributes to Muck Olla—most likely an old Celtic god. Many of those going abroad on this night lighted their way with a jack-o'-lantern, a carved turnip set aglow by a candle burning within; in Irish tradition, a fellow named Jack wanders endlessly between heaven and hell, carrying a turnip lantern lit with a piece of coal thrown to him by the devil.

Many Halloween customs crossed the Atlantic with nineteenth-century Irish immigrants to the United States, as evidenced by the American jack-o'-lanterns—carved from New World pumpkins rather than Irish turnips—at far left. As old beliefs faded in the new country, however, the use of spells and divinatory charms dwindled. Guising and begging, now called trick-or-treating, were left to the children, who still go from door to door on Halloween night, asking for the food offerings that in ancient times were lovingly prepared for the dead.

In a nineteenth-century engraving (right) of a Samhain ritual, a Celtic priest harvests mistletoe from a tree to keep ghosts at bay.

28 OCTOBER

Mistaken identities. *Today is the feast day of Saints Simon and Jude, two of Christ's apostles who have been incorrectly identified with Christian villains of similar names. People often linked Simon with Simeon—known in Italy as a goblin—and Jude with the traitor Judas. The proximity of their feast to All Souls' Day contributed to the mislaid diabolical associations. Yearly rains on the saints' day are thought to have altered history by interfering with well-laid plans.*

29 OCTOBER

A dream fulfilled. *On this date in 1929, the devastating stock market crash described in the headlines below ushered in the Great Depression— and fulfilled a prophecy by American seer Edgar Cayce. That March, a stockbroker had asked Cayce to interpret a dream in which a bull followed a woman in a red dress. Cayce said the red dress meant danger for the rising, or "bullish," market and predicted a "great disturbance in financial circles."*

30 OCTOBER

A Martian invasion. *Long before the UFO sightings of the post-World War II era, a radio play based on H. G. Wells's novel War of the Worlds and produced by Orson Welles (below) created panic on this date in 1938. Fleeing listeners, convinced that Martians had invaded New Jersey, had to be coaxed into returning home.*

31 OCTOBER

Death of a magician. *On this date in 1926, stage magician Harry Houdini (shown below with rabbits and birds used in his act) died of peritonitis. Although the legendary escape artist and conjurer was a skeptic who had exposed several fraudulent mediums, he had promised his wife, Bess, that if his spirit survived death he would try to send her a message in their secret code. Bess attended séances for many years in hopes of receiving the message, which never came.*

THE WEATHER
Rain today and probably tomorrow; somewhat colder tomorrow.

TWO CENTS

STOCK PRICES SLUMP $14,000,000,000 IN NATION-WIDE STAMPEDE TO UNLOAD; BANKERS TO SUPPORT MARKET TODAY

1 NOVEMBER

All Saints' Day. *In AD 835, the Catholic church proclaimed this All Saints' Day, a time to commemorate the holy men and women who had passed on to their heavenly rewards. As centuries passed, however, the day never shed completely its identification with the pagan festivals that had preceded it. Bonfires blazed to light the souls of the dead toward heaven, and church bells tolled as a safeguard against evil. In Spanish-speaking countries, the feast came to be called the Day of the Dead. Families remembered their departed by strewing the graves with marigold petals (above) and offering favorite foods.*

2 NOVEMBER

All Souls' Day. *Having honored the souls already in heaven on November 1, Catholics dedicate this day to the memory of those who have not yet attained a place with their Maker. On All Souls' Day, Catholics around the world attend church, pray, and visit the graves of loved ones. In parts of England, children go "souling" from house to house, asking for the small soul cakes that are traditionally set out for the dead. In Sicily, children leave their shoes outside the windows and doors, hoping that the souls of departed family members will fill them with candy and toys.*

3 NOVEMBER

Inuit Autumn Festival. *At about this time each autumn, the Inuit people of North America observe holiday festivities culminating in a tug-of-war competition with mystical implications. Two teams take their places at opposite ends of a seal-skin rope: the Ducks, who were born in summer, and the Ptarmigans, who were born in winter. According to tradition, the outcome forecasts the weather. The winter will be mild if the Ducks are victorious, but the season will be harsh if the Ptarmigans prevail. The contest is said to represent the struggle between light and darkness.*

4 NOVEMBER

Mischief Night in Britain. *The children of England once enjoyed "lawless nights" on May Eve and Halloween. In the Puritan seventeenth century, however, this tradition was moved to the eve of Guy Fawkes Day, in honor of a historical mischief-maker who was convicted of plotting to kill the king and blow up the Parliament building. Called Mischief Night, the evening became an occasion for cheerful pranks, such as taking gates off their hinges and smashing bottles outside the windows of nervous householders. Historians see in this custom remnants of a pagan festival honoring the Lord of Death.*

The Mary Celeste's Mysterious Voyage

On November 7, 1872, the American cargo vessel *Mary Celeste* set sail from New York City for Genoa, Italy, bearing 1,700 barrels of raw alcohol. A month later, the ship was found wallowing, only slightly damaged, midway between the Azores and Portugal in the North Atlantic. The captain, Benjamin Spooner Briggs, his wife, Sarah, and their two-year-old daughter, Sophia, were missing, along with the crew of seven men.

The fate of the *Mary Celeste*'s passengers and crew has never been resolved, although for a time investigators suspected a mutiny. Indeed, the lifeboat was gone, and the ship's instruments were missing or broken. However, sea chests belonging to the crew were still on board, and the skipper was reportedly well liked by his men. Some people have blamed the disappearances on the Bermuda Triangle phenomenon, which is said to wreak havoc with navigational instruments and which has been cited as the cause of many mysterious vanishings off the eastern coast of the United States.

5 NOVEMBER

Turning the Devil's Boulder. *Under an old oak tree in the Devon village of Shebbear, England, lies a large reddish rock known as the Devil's Boulder. According to local folklore, the devil long ago flung this one-ton rock into the village square. And every year on this same evening, young men gather to fulfill a centuries-old custom. Heaving and prying with poles and crowbars (above), they turn the boulder, moving it slightly, and thereby reinvoke the magic that brings them peace and prosperity.*

6 NOVEMBER

The birth of Noah. *According to James Ussher—a seventeenth-century archbishop in Ireland who published what he believed to be an accurate chronology of biblical events—this day marked the birth of Noah, the man chosen by God to repopulate the earth in the aftermath of the great Flood.*

7 NOVEMBER

A ship vanishes. *See above.*

8 NOVEMBER

An attempt on Hitler's life. *On this date in 1939, a bomb wrecked the speaker's platform of a beer hall in Munich minutes after Adolf Hitler had departed the area. Six days earlier, Swiss astrologer Karl Ernst Krafft had warned of unusual peril to the German leader in the week to follow. Security men investigated Krafft as a possible accomplice in the bombing, but they later found it prudent to hire him to chart the future for the Nazi party.*

The Day of the Fairies

Each November, the people of ancient Ireland observed Lunantishees, a day given over to the celebration of fairies. Little is known about the festivities that marked this occasion, but it is clear from the stories that survive that fairies loomed large in the Irish folklore, as they do in the customs and beliefs of many other cultures as well. Traditions involving fairies and woodland nymphs are deeply rooted in the history of religion and mythology.

The fairies of old were plentiful and wondrously varied in their attributes. Their race included brownies, goblins, mermaids, leprechauns, pixies, elves, flower sprites, bogeymen, and light-hating gnomes. In some stories the fairies were but a few inches tall; in others they were imposing creatures of larger-than-human stature. Although these elusive beings differed greatly in appearance, most of them wore green—the better to conceal themselves in the woods.

In general, Irish fairies have been characterized as mischievous rather than malicious, but a few have been accused of such evil acts as stealing human babies. In those tales, the villains usually deposited a fairy changeling in place of the missing child. The Irish also believed that every family or clan had its own private banshee, an ancestral ghost who could be heard weeping on the days leading up to a death in the family.

Beliefs about fairies have been equally diverse in places outside Ireland. In Czechoslovakia, for example, chance meetings with wood nymphs or banshees were thought to bring peril of madness. In Scotland, fairies were regarded more kindly: They were *daoine sithe,* or "men of peace." But even these gentle souls were often kidnapped by the devil in Highland lore. English tradition held that the fairy world was not inaccessible to humans. It was believed that if two people chanced to step together into a fairy ring—a round patch of bright green grass—the entire fairy universe would be rendered visible to them.

9 NOVEMBER

Loy Krathong. *On this day in Thailand, people fashion tiny boats, called krathongs, from banana and lotus leaves. When night falls, they load the boats with candles, incense, coins, and gardenia flowers, then set them adrift on a river, making wishes as the vessels drift away. Tradition holds that if the candle in a krathong stays lit until the boat is out of sight, the wish will come true. In Thailand's larger cities this practice is carried out as part of an elaborate river festival (below).*

10 NOVEMBER

Descartes' dream. *On this night in 1619, French mathematician René Descartes was disturbed by a vivid dream in which he perceived that science and philosophy should be one and the same. In the course of his lifetime, he would cement his reputation by developing a rational, scientific approach to philosophy.*

11 NOVEMBER

Martinmas. *Citizens of ancient Greece and Rome observed the feast of Vinalia on this day, honoring Bacchus, the god of wine. By medieval times, the Catholic church had tamed the feast to some extent by drawing it into the Christian calendar. Since that time, the day has been called Martinmas in honor of Saint Martin, patron of vintners and tavern keepers. Tradition teaches that the weather on this day provides a clue to the harshness of the coming winter: A bright and sunny Martinmas bodes for icy weather, but frost before this date means a mild winter ahead.*

12 NOVEMBER

The Haitian Yam Festival. *When the yam crop is ready to be harvested, the farmers of Haiti honor their ancestors who brought yams from Africa to the West Indies. As part of their observances, the Haitians seek good fortune for the next year's crop by offering bowls of cut-up yams to their forebears, starting with those relatives who have died most recently. Offerings are then made to the household gods before the yams are thrown into a pot, cooked with fish, and eaten.*

[Hindu...] ...in their homes, with a broom, a *[...]* festoon *[...]* rice paste and earth pigment. Such decorations are thought to bring good fortune during the annual festival called Diwali.

13 NOVEMBER

A great meteor shower. *On the night of November 13, 1866, people throughout Europe witnessed a dazzling meteor shower. "The heavens seemed alive," wrote a reporter for the Times of London. "It seemed as if a mighty wind had caught the old stars, loosed them from their holdings, and swept them across the firmament." Although the journalist who made these observations understood the natural phenomenon that had caused the display, some of his contemporaries were firmly convinced that the meteors were transport for celestial visitors.*

14 NOVEMBER

Ritual demands. *Among the Alaskan Inuit tribes, this day marks the start of the Asking Festival, an annual sharing of the wealth. On the first night, youths go door to door soliciting for food for a huge community feast. The next night, everyone gathers to ask one another for gifts of personal property. It is considered bad manners to refuse a request, so at the end of the evening people go home laden with their neighbors' possessions.*

15 NOVEMBER

Seven-Five-Three. *For the annual festival of Shichi-Go-San in Japan, children who have attained their seventh, fifth, or third birthdays follow their parents to a Shinto shrine to offer thanks for their continued good health. At the end of the ceremony, the priests drop "thousand-year" candies into the children's bags, which have been decorated with good luck signs (below).*

16 NOVEMBER

Diwali. *Each year at about this time the people of India celebrate Diwali, the Festival of Lights. This vibrant five-day event marks the Hindu New Year and is considered an auspicious time to honor Lakshmi, goddess of wealth and prosperity. To ensure that Lakshmi will feel welcome in their homes, celebrants scrub their houses and light an array of candles.*

A Past Life Revealed

On a November night in 1952, Virginia Tighe, a twenty-nine-year-old mother of three in Pueblo, Colorado, was under hypnosis for an experiment in regression when she declared that she had lived in Ireland more than a century earlier as Bridget "Bridey" Murphy. Her hypnotist, Morey Bernstein, induced further trances at later dates in which Tighe described nineteenth-century Irish life in remarkable detail. She named shops she allegedly had frequented in Belfast and used colloquial terms for everyday items, such as "platters" for potato cakes. Questioned under trance about the long interval that passed between her two lives, she told of being in "a place of waiting . . . where everybody waits," until she "passed into another existence."

Tighe had apparently never visited Ireland, and Bernstein professed to be equally lacking in knowledge of that country. Investigators later corroborated much of what Tighe had revealed under hypnosis, making hers one of the most tantalizingly believable tales of reincarnation.

17 NOVEMBER

Sending the winter dress. *On the first day of the tenth month of the Chinese calendar—around mid-November by Western lights—families in some parts of China observe the last of three yearly festivals of death. Following the ancient belief that the dead need protection from the chill of winter, they make paper garments and pack them along with a little money in parcels labeled with the recipients' names. The parcels are "delivered" through burning, which symbolically sends them to the world of the ancestors.*

18 NOVEMBER

A tight-maneuvering UFO. *On this night in 1948, an air force pilot flying over Andrews Air Force Base in Maryland spotted a glowing white object crossing the sky. He turned to investigate but found that the object swerved abruptly away. A series of dogfight twists and turns ensued in which the pilot attempted to put the object between his craft and the light of nearby Washington, D.C. With every attempt, however, the UFO evaded him, showing remarkable maneuverability. Ultimately, the UFO escaped, but witnesses on the ground corroborated the pilot's description of a wingless, oval object with a solitary light.*

19 NOVEMBER

Bridey Murphy emerges. *See above.*

20 NOVEMBER

Makahiki. *At about this time each November, the native people of Hawaii mark the start of their harvest season, Makahiki. Rituals and celebrations commence when the cluster of stars called the Pleiades becomes visible, inching its way along the horizon. According to tradition, war is forbidden during this season, and special reverence is due to the god Lono.*

Sagittarius: November 22–December 20

The period of the astrological year that falls under the sign of Sagittarius begins on November 22 and runs through December 20. The symbol of this ninth sign of the zodiac is the Sagittarian Centaur, an archer who is half man, half horse. The Centaur represents the harmonious union of the physical and spiritual components of human beings. Sagittarians, astrologers say, have the potential to meld the two elements.

People born under the sign are said to be idealistic, optimistic, and enthusiastic. Ruled by Jupiter, they take on the confidence and sense of justice of that Roman king of the gods. Insatiably curious, Sagittarians detest sameness, constantly questing after new experiences. Their zodiacal sign is thought to rule the hips and thighs—parts of the body essential to movement—and astrologers say that Sagittarians walk the globe driven by an insatiable wanderlust. If they are not free to roam, they often turn inward, plumbing the depths of their imaginations. In either case, however, the journey itself usually proves more fulfilling than the destination, which frequently disappoints them.

With their boundless zeal and sanguine outlook, Sagittarians may launch into more projects than they can finish. And, in their well-meaning but blundering expansiveness, they tend toward exaggeration, carelessness, and tactlessness. Famous Sagittarians include singer Frank Sinatra, cinematographer Woody Allen, and actress Jane Fonda.

21 NOVEMBER

A god's annual visit. *Every year at this time, a Mayan festival lasting several days culminated in the anticipated descent from heaven by the god Kukulcan. By way of preparation, the Mayans fasted, burned incense, made offerings of food, and created brilliant banners of colored feathers. But on the day of the deity's supposed arrival, pious work gave way to joyful merrymaking.*

22 NOVEMBER

A predicted assassination. *On November 22, 1963, President John Fitzgerald Kennedy was assassinated on a street in Dallas, Texas. Six months earlier, American astrologer Leslie McIntyre had warned in a magazine article that certain astrological configurations indicated "personal danger to our head of State" at about this date.*

23 NOVEMBER

The festival of smiths. *On this day, the people of England remember Saint Clement, who was martyred by drowning, having been tied to an anchor. He thus became the patron of ironworkers, who marked his day with elaborate rituals. Historians believe that the feast probably falls on the date of a much earlier rite for the wizard-blacksmith of the Saxon gods.*

24 NOVEMBER

Good luck rakes. *In late November, Japan celebrates Tori-No-Ichi and begins preparations for New Year. A token of this festival is the kumade (below), a bamboo rake adorned with good luck symbols to help its bearer "rake in" good fortune.*

25 NOVEMBER

Age of Aquarius begins. *By late November in 1967, the cast of the newly opened rock musical Hair was proclaiming to packed houses the "dawning of the Age of Aquarius." A new era of peace, understanding, and happiness had been projected by many astrologers.*

26 NOVEMBER

Basari initiation rites. *Each autumn at about this time, fifteen-year-old boys in the Basari villages of Senegal are ceremonially welcomed to manhood. Before making this passage, the youths undergo many months of preparation and various tests of their ingenuity and adaptability. At one point, they must fend for themselves for several days in the bush without provisions carried from home. They must also observe a month of total silence, while going about their business in the villages. When the time for adulthood arrives, however, they can sing, dance, and show off their strength among the other men in their communities.*

27 NOVEMBER

Gujeswari Jatra. *On the tenth day of the waning moon in late November or early December, Buddhists and Hindus of Nepal hold an annual festival in honor of the powerful mother goddess Gujeswari. All day long, devotees bring offerings to the temple of the deity, which was built around an ancient spring in the Katmandu Valley. There they pray before the kalash, a sacred water vessel made of red clay. In the evening, celebrants carry a copy of the kalash in a musical procession that winds its way through the neighboring towns.*

28 NOVEMBER

Birth of William Blake. *The great English poet, painter, engraver, and mystic William Blake was born on this day in 1757. Blake declared that he was always guided in his work by unseen spirits who "dictated" to him the contents of his poetry. Of his visionary poem Milton, he said, "I may praise it, since I dare not pretend to be other than the Secretary; the Authors are in Eternity." He rejected the rationalism and materialism of his century, arguing that truth could be found only in the imagination. "To me," he said, "this world is all one continued vision of fancy or imagination."*

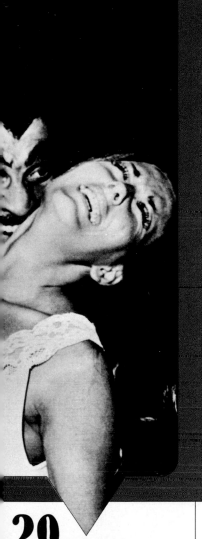

Patron Saint of Scotland—and Love

The Roman Catholic church designated November 30 as the feast of Saint Andrew, who—like his brother Peter—was a fisherman and one of the original Twelve Apostles. Andrew was said to have been crucified in Greece on an X-shaped cross like the one shown here. Somehow he supposedly was buried in Scotland and became the patron saint of that realm. To this day, the feast is celebrated there with parades and local fairs.

Andrew was renowned for his gentle and loving manner, so it was perhaps not surprising when traditions arose that made Saint Andrew's Day into a special time for love omens and charms. In Czechoslovakia, young women performed a ritual in which they pulled sticks at random out of their woodpiles. A crooked stick, custom dictated, forecast marriage to a hunchback; a straight one promised a husband who was slim and tall. In Hungary, the favored method for divining one's mate was to pour melted lead through the handle of a key and catch it in a glass of water. The shape assumed by the cooling metal would supposedly reveal the occupation of the husband-to-be.

29 NOVEMBER

Vampire Night. *On this night in Rumania, strigoii, or vampires, are said to rise from their tombs and seek out their former homes. Women hang garlic on doors and windows to keep out the evil beings. If the vampires fail to find unprotected victims, some say, they fight among themselves before returning to their graves for another year.*

30 NOVEMBER

Priest and witch? *In November 1634, Father Urbain Grandier, a sexually and politically indiscreet French cleric, was arrested on trumped-up charges of bewitching a whole convent of nuns. The evidence against him—a letter purportedly signed by demons—was clearly a forgery, but the priest's enemies saw to it that he was burned alive.*

Heralding the New Year

"Man," wrote British classical scholar Gilbert Murray, "longs for a new life, a new age, with young gods, not stained by the deaths and impurities of the past." Since earliest times, people have sought to satisfy this deep-rooted yearning for re-creation by celebrating the New Year. Observed on varying dates in different lands, New Year festivals mark the pivotal point where time is deemed to begin anew, and the world and individuals alike can emerge pure and pristine—if the proper steps are taken.

First, celebrants must banish the past's malicious spirits and accumulat-

In a swirling blur of vibrant colors, Buddhist monks expel the sinister spirits of the past with their Black Hat Dance. Masks, such as that of the skull-

ed evils to prevent their infecting the coming year. Next come rites of purification, followed by positive acts to ensure an auspicious future. Sometimes participants are unaware they are following ancient mystical practices: Few Westerners, for instance, realize that their New Year horns and fireworks were once meant to drive away evil spirits.

But some old rituals survive in their full significance. An example is Tibetan Buddhism's new year, known as Losar, a five-day festival that often falls in early February. The vigor of that celebration is evidence that such annual rites of renewal still have a powerful grip on human feelings.

Tibetan men sound huge horns to scare evil away from the new year (above). Indoors, houses are swept to rid them of dust-lurking demons.

festooned god Mahakala (top), are often worn during this dramatic Losar ritual—a reenactment of the conflict between good and evil.

Sporting yellow coxcomb hats worn for religious festivals, Tibetan monks in India erect an ornate wooden model crowned with a skull-like head on which they will confer the sins and evils of the past year. When this sacrificial object is later set ablaze during the purification ceremonies of Losar, the faithful believe their faults are burned up with the effigy, enabling them to enter the new year untarnished.

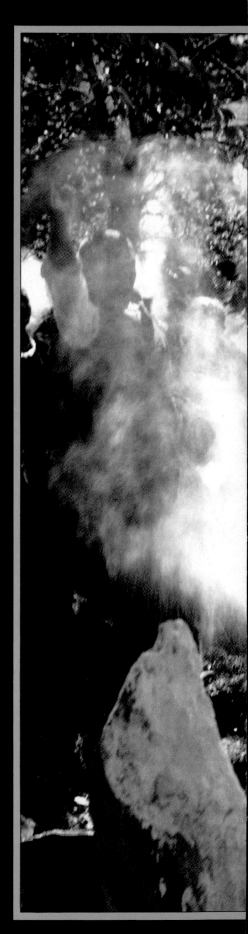

"Victory to the gods," shout Losar celebrants as they hurl fistfuls of powdered grain known as tsampa into the air, a purifying ritual thought to cast away evil and attract good luck. In some Tibetan households during Losar, family members are rubbed with a ball of tsampa dough. According to tradition, the dough ball extracts any troubling physical or spiritual pains or ailments, so that the person being rubbed can begin the new year with a clean bill of health.

In a Losar ceremony intended to promote good fortune in the coming year, Tibetan Buddhist monks living in India splash white barley beer known as chang into overflowing chalices as an offering to the gods. Celebrants believe another means of securing an auspicious future is drinking directly from a source of water—a river, lake, spring, or pond—at sunrise on the first day of the new year. At home, Tibetans drink warm chang to celebrate Losar, another custom that is thought to draw favor to the infant year.

A smiling monk distributes strips of cloth blessed by the Dalai Lama—the holy leader of Tibetan Buddhism—to an eager crowd of the faithful during Losar festivities. Because the sacred scraps are thought to bring good luck, many Tibetans wear them around their necks or display them in their homes for the rest of the year. Marking the front door with a swastika, the ancient mystical sign of luck and eternity, is another tradition believed to lure favorable fortune to one's house as the new year commences.

Buddhist shrine in Nepal, banners printed with prayers in praise of the gods dance in the wind, which is believed to carry the messages to heaven. Every year near the end of Losar, Buddhists replace the prayer flags that stream from temples, houses, and even trees throughout their lands. Offering a prayer flag at this time is thought to ensure a propitious year for the donor and the donor's family.

Winter

Winter in the northern lands is a season of contradictions—a fact reflected in the unusually varied festivals and mystic happenings illustrated in the pages that follow. While the last dead leaves cling to windblown branches, life stirs anew in seeds under the frozen earth; with nights at their longest, the sun begins its slow but inevitable return. And, as the season wears on, the tedium of chill and damp gives way to joy at the turning of the year toward warmth and light.

Turquoise is December's talisman. Legend tells that the stone protects one from injury in a fall by attracting the force of the impact to itself.

In ages past, people escaped winter storms to warm themselves by smoky fires, listening to the sagas of heroes, gods, and other uncanny beings. Winter itself became a storm god, or a series of ice and snow spirits, while the sparkling ice transmuted into fierce Norse frost giants and other frost spirits. In northerly climes, such spirits were feared and respected, honored with regular sacrifices to protect livestock and early plantings.

Still more fearsome entities—ghosts and evil spirits—have traditionally found the dim chill of winter a congenial time to stalk the earth; appeasing them or driving them away has been an important aspect of winter festivals since the time of ancient Greece. Many Chinese winter rituals commemorate the dead, as does the European assumption that family ghosts may return on Christmas Eve.

January's birthstone is the garnet, a symbol of constancy. Worn to a wedding, it is said to attract a husband; as a gift, it wins the affection of the recipient.

For all the attention to the dead, however, some winter holidays celebrate the impending return of life with feasts and revelry that are unmatched in other seasons. In the fourth century, a Greek writer named Libanius described the city of Antioch's winter festival in terms reminiscent of a modern Christmas. "There is food everywhere, heavy, rich food, and laughter. A positive urge to spend seizes on everyone," he wrote. "The streets are full of people and coaches, staggering under the load of gifts. Children are free of the dread of their teachers, and for slaves the festival is as good as a holiday." The joyous mood of that ancient Greek feast time appears in winter festivals the world over, from the colorful dragon floats of the Chinese New Year parades to the extravagant costumes of Carnival dancers in Rio de Janeiro. Such rites offer continuing proof that not even winter's gloom can quench the human spirit or obscure the certain knowledge that spring and new life will one day reappear.

Amethyst is special to the month of February. The ancients believed that the purple stone prevented intoxication and guarded against poison, pain, and plague.

1 DECEMBER

Beginning of Advent. *See below left.*

Advent—Making Ready for Christmas

Advent, the first season of the Christian ecclesiastical year, contains the four Sundays immediately preceding Christmas, traditionally represented by the four candles on wreaths like the one above. In past times, it was observed with great austerities: Fasting was ordained, church organs remained silent for the first two Sundays, and marriages were prohibited throughout the period.

Folk customs did not always match the Church's severity. In Rome, the last days of Advent were celebrated by Calabrian *pifferari*, bagpipers who swarmed through the city, playing at shrines of the Virgin Mary. Their music was meant to recall that of the shepherds who, according to tradition, visited the baby Jesus and played such pipes.

During Advent in Normandy, farmers sent their children, armed with flaming torches, to drive away pests. Only children younger than twelve were believed innocent enough to perform this service, which involved setting fire to bundles of hay, lighting piles of straw placed under trees, and chanting to banish mice, caterpillars, and moles.

In other regions, Advent was a time for a girl to divine the name of her future husband. Taking a number of onions, she carved on each the name of a fancied spouse, then placed the onions near the fire. The name engraved on whichever onion sprouted first was the boy she would marry.

Poor women in some parts of England carried a pair of dolls during the last week in Advent, one dressed as Jesus and one as Mary. Everyone to whom they showed the dolls was expected to contribute a halfpenny, or risk a dose of bad luck.

2 DECEMBER

Whirling in prayer. *At about this time of year, Turkey celebrates a festival of whirling dervishes, Sufi mystics like the one shown above who open themselves to the Divine with their spinning dances.*

Homage to an ancient tree. *Around this date, Buddhist pilgrims pay their respects to the world's oldest documented tree (below, behind fence), planted in 288 BC as an offshoot of the tree under which the Buddha attained enlightenment.*

3 DECEMBER

Rites for the Good Goddess. *On this day, the vestal virgins of ancient Rome conducted secret ceremonies, from which males were barred, for Bona Dea, the Good Goddess. When a rash young man named Publius Clodius tricked Julius Caesar's wife Pompeia into allowing him near the ceremony in 61 BC, his discovery caused a great scandal. Tradition has it that Caesar divorced Pompeia at once, not because he thought her guilty but because "Caesar's wife must be above suspicion."*

4 DECEMBER

Theosophy meets the arts. *Wassily Kandinsky was born on this date in 1866. An influential modern painter, the Russian Kandinsky blended the mysticism of Rudolf Steiner, Helena Petrovna Blavatsky, and Annie Besant into a new theory of painting that incorporated "thought vibrations" and "spiritual atmosphere" in ways that only those who were spiritually initiated could fully understand.*

5 DECEMBER

Flight 19 disappears. *On this day in 1945, fourteen crew members in five U.S. Navy Avenger bombers like the ones shown below took off from Fort Lauderdale, Florida, for a training flight; none were heard from again. Some investigators speculated the crew members were victims of the Bermuda Triangle. Others believed them snapped up by a UFO. In May 1991, treasure hunters using sonar discovered five Avengers on the seabed several miles off the Florida coast, but further investigation showed they were not the missing planes.*

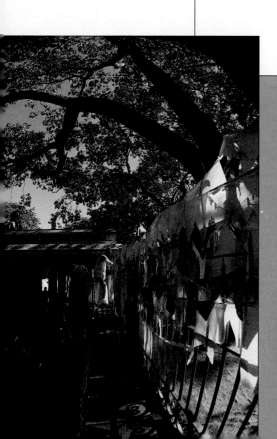

In this ivory carving, hunters arrive at a hole in the ice with the bladders of sea mammals dangling from poles. They stab and sink the organs, thereby allegedly freeing the animals' spirits.

6 DECEMBER

The original Santa Claus. *Nicholas, a fourth-century bishop in Turkey, reportedly saved three girls from being sold into slavery by their destitute father. He anonymously gave them three bags of gold, thus enabling them to marry honorably. Because legend says he also brought back to life three murdered schoolboys, he is considered a patron of youth. This day of his death is remembered in many European countries as Saint Nicholas Day, with festivals (above) in which children receive gifts in accord with their behavior during the year. Through a Dutch abbreviation, Sinterklaas, he became Santa Claus, the jolly benefactor who brings Christmas gifts to children.*

7 DECEMBER

Royal Air Force spirit. *On December 7, 1918, Lt. David McConnell left Scampton, England, to ferry a plane to a nearby base. Shortly before 3:30 p.m., his roommate, Lt. Larkin, heard McConnell say, "Hullo, boy!" and looked up to see him at the door. "Back already?" Larkin asked. "Yes," McConnell said, "had a good trip." He left. Minutes later another officer came by, seeking McConnell; Larkin said he had just left the room. They later learned McConnell had died in a crash sixty miles away at 3:25 p.m.—around the time Larkin spoke with him. The case became noted for the veracity of the witnesses.*

8 DECEMBER

A goddess's natal day. *Japanese Shintoists celebrate the birth of their sun goddess, Amaterasu (below), on this day. According to ancient mythology, the goddess dwells in a heavenly realm much like Japan. But there is little harmony in her blessed land because she does not get along with her brother, the moon god, who also lives there. The feuding pair sit with their backs to each other, creating, say the Shintoists, the division between night and day.*

9 DECEMBER

An American first. *On this day in 1792, the first formal cremation of a colonial American—statesman Henry Laurens—took place in South Carolina. Today, cremation is still the exception in much of the Western world, most likely because of an old taboo. Early Christians associated the act with paganism and feared it might impede resurrection and eternal life. In Great Britain, however, more than half those who die are now cremated.*

Rites of the Arctic Night

Among Inuit of the far north, hunters idled by the prolonged darkness of the Arctic winter traditionally held December ceremonies to propitiate the souls of the animals they had killed in the preceding year. At Saint Michael in Alaska, in a common building called the *kashim*, hunters would undergo five days of purification rites involving the inflated bladders of all the animals they had killed that year—seals, whales, walruses, and polar bears. At the end of the five days, under the full moon, the men would cut a hole in the sea ice about a quarter mile from shore and the next day would thrust the consecrated bladders into the frigid water. On returning to the village, they would be greeted by all the people around a bonfire. After the men had leaped through the flame, they would return to the kashim for a final sweat bath and contests of strength.

10 DECEMBER

The Bladder Festival. *See above.*

11 DECEMBER

A fateful trio of omens. *On this day in 1825, Russian poet Alexander Pushkin had planned to visit some friends in Saint Petersburg. As he made ready to go, however, first one rabbit, then another scooted across his path. The animals portended bad luck, Pushkin believed, but he was reluctant to cancel his trip. He headed out of town, only to have a black-clad priest cross in front of his carriage—a third foreboding of doom. Frightened, Pushkin turned for home, and he later learned that two of the friends he had intended to visit had been hanged in a political upheaval.*

12 DECEMBER

Fire and water. *The Zoroastrian festival of Sada is celebrated in Iran at about this time with a huge bonfire built near a body of water. Kindled as the sun sets, the blaze represents the victories of light over darkness and of good over evil.*

13 DECEMBER

Saint Lucia's Day. *In the dark of winter in Sweden, this day is celebrated as a festival of light. (The saint's name is derived from the Latin word for light.) The eldest daughter of each family, dressed in white and crowned with pine twigs festooned with candles (above), brings coffee to her parents in bed. She is later accorded a place of honor at breakfast in a brightly lit room.*

Guadalupe's Holy Protector

In 1531, the Virgin Mary appeared in Guadalupe, near Mexico City, to a woodcutter named Juan Diego, an Indian convert to Catholicism. She asked him to tell the bishop of Mexico City to build a shrine on that spot, so she could protect the poor Indians of the land. When the bishop asked for proof, the Virgin appeared again to Juan Diego, bidding him fill his rough blanket with roses he would find growing out of season. When he opened the flower-laden blanket before the bishop on December 12, an image of the Virgin appeared on it. The bishop had a chapel built, and the blanket picture has hung there since, except during a flood in 1629, when the archbishop took a boat to the church and brought the picture back to his cathedral. The end of the flood was credited to Our Lady of Guadalupe. Today worshipers flock to the chapel *(right)* on the anniversary of the picture's appearance.

14 December

Hopi rites of winter. *The Hopi of what is now the southwestern United States celebrate the return of life to the world with Soyal, a month-long ceremony beginning on the new moon before the shortest day of the year. The major rites, usually eight days before the solstice, include a celebration of creation and rebirth dedicated to Spider Woman and Hawk Maiden. To ensure the return of the sun, a failed mock attack is made against the holder of a sun shield like the one below, dramatizing the sun's eventual victory over winter darkness.*

15 December

The Yuletide Lads. *These mischief makers are thirteen impish creatures who visit Icelandic homes, one each day from December 12 through Christmas Eve. Descendants of Gryla the Ogre in Icelandic mythology, the Lads were once considered cannibals, but they are now viewed more benignly as gift-bearing spirits friendly to children. Their remaining tendency to mischief, however, is reflected in the Lads' individual names, which range from Sausage Sniffer and Pot Scraper to Window Peeper.*

16 December

Death of Hildegard of Bingen. *In 1179, after a long life of visions and faith healing, Hildegard of Bingen, depicted in the medieval illumination above, died in her cloister at Rupertsberg in Germany. She had cured and counseled pilgrims from across Europe, and on the night she died, the stars were said to have formed a cross, a sign that the heavens accepted her gladly.*

17 December

Saturnalia. *See below.*

Capricorn: December 21-January 19

Capricorn begins on the first day of winter, as life is enmeshed in a struggle for survival. Ruled by Saturn, the planet of rationality, and Uranus, the planet of will power, natives of Capricorn tend to a cool detachment that allows a supremely logical view of reality.

Capricorn's totem is the goat, an animal that may be domesticated and tethered, or may roam freely on mountain peaks. Natives of the sign who feel shackled by responsibility are aloof and austere plodders, flawlessly reliable but seldom cheerful. Capricorns who blaze their own trails, however, cultivate a resiliency and black humor that help them achieve their goals.

Capricorns have plenty of ambition, as well as great powers of concentration that allow them to keep their eyes on long-term success despite the distraction of brilliant but fleeting victories. Obstacles never deter them, at worst only slowing their climb: Stubborn as their animal totem, Capricorns are willing to suffer privation and sacrifice as they follow their dreams.

Those born under this sign risk isolating themselves from others because of their solitary nature, and they may end up reaching the pinnacles of success only to find themselves alone. Ultimately, however, their attitude toward other human beings is often one of indifference. Somewhat dispassionate in their relationships, they may disappoint lovers who seek caring interaction. And although they command the respect of their peers, they rarely inspire affection.

Celebrated Capricorns include actress Mary Tyler Moore, boxer Muhammad Ali, and singer David Bowie.

18 DECEMBER

Greetings to four brothers. *In traditional Latvian homes, this winter festival hails the return of light and the birth of God, called Diev. The heralds of the solstice are the Four Brothers Ziemassvētki, celestial beings bearing gifts. Latvians decorate their houses gaily in preparation for Ziemassvētki and lay in many different kinds of food for the feasts that accompany the four-day celebration.*

19 DECEMBER

The goddess of success. *On the third day of the Saturnalia, Romans celebrated Opalia, in honor of Ops, the wife of Saturn and the goddess of fertility and success.*

20 DECEMBER

Halcyon days. *Contrary to the season's typical blustery weather, the weeks before and after the winter solstice—a period known as the halcyon days—are supposed to be calm and tranquil. The name is derived from the legendary halcyon, a bird sometimes identified with the kingfisher, which the ancients believed built its nest on the ocean, bearing its young in the winter. To preserve the brood from the severity of the season, the halcyon was said to calm wind and waves with its song.*

21 DECEMBER

The sun enters the sign of Capricorn. *See above.*

When Slaves Became Their Masters' Masters

In ancient Roman times, people put away work and war for a brief time every December during Saturnalia, a week-long festival honoring the god Saturn *(left)*. Because the autumn plowing and sowing were done, bringing the year's agricultural work to a close, countryfolk were particularly joyous during Saturnalia. Even in the city, however, Saturnalia was a period of complete relaxation and uninhibited merrymaking.

No public business could be transacted, courts and schools were closed, wars were suspended, and all feuds were held in abeyance.

Throughout this period between the death of the old year and the birth of the new, a kind of chaos reigned. Slaves wore their masters' clothes and sat at their tables; masters waited upon slaves, who could berate them as they wished. In the eastern province, lots were cast to choose a mock king

who issued comic orders. Some have speculated that this figure may have been the relic of a darker ceremony in which a young man was selected to rule briefly in the king's stead, only to be sacrificed on an altar at the winter solstice to ensure the return of spring. In Rome itself, another symbolic act—the exchange of special wax tapers called *cerei*—was believed to ensure the return of light after the winter solstice.

The Many Faces of Christmas

Although it now celebrates the birth of Jesus, Christmas has its roots in holidays far more ancient and retains strong traces of pagan festivals incorporated as Christianity spread across Europe and the world. Before the fourth century, December 25 in Rome was the date of the Mithraic Dies Natalis Invicti Solis—Birthday of the Unconquered Sun. The cult of Mithras was the leading competitor to Christianity in Rome; followers of Mithras—who is shown at far right sacrificing a bull—identified their god with the sun and his birthday with the winter solstice. The early Church converted the birthday into one more suitable for Christians to celebrate.

Dies Natalis Invicti Solis was a purely religious holiday, more important to priests than to the masses. Christmas, however,

22 DECEMBER

Winter solstice. *For ancient farmers, dependent on the sun for their very lives, the shortest day of the year, which occurs at about this time, was a day of celebration: Henceforth, days would grow progressively longer. To ensure that this annual shift out of cold and darkness did in fact come to pass, the farmers performed ceremonies designed to induce the sun to return. Sympathetic magic played a large role in these rites and survives in the practices of tribal cultures and witches. Dances, chants, sexual license, elaborate miming, and verbal formulas all had their part. Bonfires were often used to encourage the sun and to drive off evil.*

23 DECEMBER

Festival for a divine guest. *The Kalash, an isolated tribe in the high valleys of the Hindu Kush, dress in their finest (below) to celebrate Chaomos, a week-long festival honoring the demigod Balomain, who counts the Kalash each year and carries their prayers back to Tsiam, their mythical ancestral home.*

24 DECEMBER

Christmas Eve ghosts. *Like other Europeans, the Finns still associate ghosts with Christmas Eve, one of the longest nights of the year. As shown below, many set out candles at the graves of family members to light the path of ancestral spirits as they make their annual visit home.*

25 DECEMBER

Christmas Day. *See above.*

soon took on aspects of the Saturnalia festivities, and as Christianity spread, other folk traditions and pagan rituals found their way into the celebration. One particularly durable solstice festival was Jol (Yule), a feast celebrated all over northern Europe in honor of Jolnir—another name for Odin, chief among the Norse gods.

Since Odin was the god of intoxicating drink and ecstasy as well as the god of death, Yule customs varied widely. Odin's sacrificial beer became the specially blessed Christmas beer mentioned in medieval laws; fresh food and drink were left on tables after Christmas feasts, to feed roaming Yuletide ghosts. Even the bonfires of old survived in the tradition of the Yule log, a selected tree trunk that varied in size and type but that

always brought luck to the house where it was burned.

Christmas incorporated many other pagan customs. Holly and ivy, for instance, sacred to the ancient gods Saturn and Dionysus, were believed to have magic power against evil. Even the Christmas tree *(far left)*, which came into common use only in nineteenth-century Germany, is perhaps a throwback to a great tree from Norse mytholo-gy that was named Ygg-drasil.

26 DECEMBER

Two rare days off. *Bahamians celebrate the Junkanoo festival on this day and January 1 with music, costumes, and dance. In the era of slavery, the two Junkanoo days were among very few times when slaves were not required to work. Their revelry harked back to their African origins, and the name of the festival may derive from the French "gens inconnus," or "the unknown," a possible reference to the elaborately made up and garbed marchers who parade accompanied by the music of drums, bells, whistles, and conch shells through the predawn darkness.*

27 DECEMBER

Guarding against poisoners. *On this date is celebrated the Feast of Saint John, who safely drank poisoned wine after making the sign of the cross over it; some seek protection against poison by drinking blessed wine on this day.*

A warrior goddess. *The birth of the Norse goddess Freya was celebrated at this time. Often depicted astride a large cat (below), she gathered to her palace warriors slain in battle.*

28 DECEMBER

A gathering of gods. *On Ta Chiu, a festival of peace and renewal celebrated at about this time, Taoist temples in Hong Kong combine to summon all their gods and ghosts to one place, where people make offerings. At the end of the festival, priests read a list of names of all the people in the area. The list is attached to a paper horse and set afire, so the names rise to heaven with the smoke.*

29 DECEMBER

Miracle of the lights. *Hanukkah, the Jewish Festival of Lights, which is observed during this period, commemorates the rededication of the Temple in Jerusalem after the expulsion of the Syrians in 165 BC. The Syrians had profaned the Temple by erecting heathen altars within. After it was purified and the perpetual flame was relit, only one jar of sacred oil remained, enough for only a single day. But, miraculously, the flame burned for eight days. Jewish families observe the eight-day festival of Hanukkah by lighting one additional candle each night on a special candelabrum called a menorah.*

30 DECEMBER

A strange exorcism. *The offices of a British charlatan named Simon Forman, born on this day in 1552, consisted of a room for wart reading and breast massage, one for marital guidance, and one for the practice of magical arts. It was likely in the last chamber that Forman began his treatment of a knight reportedly plagued by worms in the nose. Convinced that the parasites were demons in disguise, the doctor administered a so-called demonifuge medicine. He then rubbed the knight down with heavy stones and, at midnight, immersed him headfirst in a stagnant frog pond. According to all reports, the treatment worked.*

31 DECEMBER

Japanese demons. *On the eve of the new year, straw-clad young men called Namahage (below) descend on the villages of the Oga Peninsula in northeastern Japan. Representing spirits determined to drive out misfortune and ensure a rich harvest for the coming year, the bellowing demons storm from house to house, searching for children, single women, and young brides. "Are there naughty children here? Does the new bride sleep late in the morning?" the Namahage demand to know. Householders appease the demons with sake, and with a final outburst, they depart. A Namahage follower collects donations of money and rice cakes.*

1 JANUARY

Panicked millennialists. *Convinced that the world was about to end as the first millennium drew to a close, frightened Christians throughout Europe gathered to pray for mercy on this day in AD 1000. Some of them even undertook pilgrimages to Jerusalem to attend the Second Coming of Christ. Life returned to normal, however, when the day passed uneventfully.*

An auspicious inauguration. *On this day in 1967, Ronald Reagan (below) was sworn in as governor of California at sixteen minutes past midnight—a time that some believe was chosen for him by an astrologer.*

2 JANUARY

Cosmic goddess. *This date marks the birth of Inanna, Sumerian queen of heaven and earth.*

How January 1 Became New Year's Day

Ancient Egyptians, Phoenicians, and Persians proclaimed the start of a new year on the autumnal equinox, September 22; early Greeks observed the occasion first at the winter solstice, December 21, later at the summer solstice, June 21. It was not until 153 BC, with the reformation of the Roman calendar, that the first day of a new year was observed on January 1. The day and the month were dedicated by the Romans to the god Janus (left), commonly shown with two faces, one regarding the year gone by and the other looking toward the year upcoming.

In Rome, the beginning of the new year was a time to expunge the ills of the past twelve months and to establish a pattern for the next twelve through good conduct. Friends reconciled their differences, adversaries suspended litigation, and people exchanged visits and gifts.

Many of these old Roman customs survive in Europe and Latin America, overlaid with new superstitions. In many places the first person to enter a house on New Year's Day is thought to determine the luck for the coming year. Bad luck is believed to accompany a woman, particularly one with fair or red hair; tall, dark-haired men are in great demand as "first-footers," supposedly bringing assurance of a happy year to come.

3 JANUARY

Sleeping prophet. *On this date in 1945 American psychic healer Edgar Cayce died. Known as the "sleeping prophet," Cayce recited more than fourteen thousand diagnoses and predictions while in a trance. He collapsed in late 1944 and in a reading for himself was told to rest "until he is well or dead." Cayce soon had a stroke that ended his life at age sixty-seven.*

Deer dancing. *To ensure fertility for the tribe's women, the Pueblo Indians of the southwestern United States don deer headdresses (below) and perform ritual dances.*

4 JANUARY

Homage to a stellar figure. *At about this time of year, some Koreans perform a ceremony called Chilseong-je, or Sacrifice to the Seven Stars. Convening at midnight, they present an offering of white rice and clean water to the seven stars that form the constellation known as Ursa Major, the Great Bear. In the Korean pantheon, the god who rules Ursa Major also has a hand in human affairs, so the people hope to earn good will by propitiating the constellation.*

5 JANUARY

Twelfth Night. *Twelfth Night heralds the end of Christmastide and the eve of Epiphany, but its celebration recalls pre-Christian traditions of reversing social rules. In medieval Europe, each cathedral ordained a bishop and archbishop of fools in parodies of real ceremonies; priests danced and sang obscene songs; deacons played cards on the altar; and worshipers jumped about the church, enjoying the ritual breach of religious taboos.*

6 JANUARY

Day of glory. *The Feast of the Epiphany celebrates three manifestations of Christ's glory: the Magi's veneration of the infant Jesus in Bethlehem; his baptism in the Jordan River; and his miracle at Cana, turning water into wine.*

Winter's fright. *In Austria, costumed villagers (below) celebrate Schemenlauf, a noisy festival of marches, dances, drumming, and bell-ringing—to scare winter away.*

Fatal Encounter with a UFO

On January 7, 1948, an unidentified flying object was spotted streaking through the sky over western Kentucky, near Godman Air Force Base. One observer described the strange shape, estimated to be 250 to 300 feet in diameter, as looking like "an ice cream cone topped with red." Three Air National Guard pilots flying Mustang fighters *(right)* saw the UFO swoop over their airfield; they were ordered to chase it.

Climbing in pursuit, the pilots glimpsed a huge, teardrop-shaped object that seemed almost fluid. Two fliers quit, but Captain Thomas Mantell radioed that he was climbing to 20,000 feet for a closer look. It was Mantell's last message; hours later his body was found in the wreckage of his plane.

Rumors spread that Mantell had been blasted from the sky by an alien spacecraft. Air force investigators had another explanation: He had been flying without oxygen and when he climbed too high he lost consciousness and spun to earth. Although investigators speculated that the object of the chase was probably a high-altitude research balloon, no one knows for sure.

7 JANUARY

Kentucky UFO sighting. *See above.*

8 JANUARY

Return to Heartbreak Hotel. *Elvis Presley was born on this date in 1935 and died on August 16, 1977—or did he? Thousands of the rock-and-roll star's fans believe Elvis lives, either as a visible spirit or in the flesh. He was buried less than two weeks when three men tried to break into his tomb to prove he was not there. Supposed new tapes of his voice and alleged photos of him have been offered as proof of his survival. And reported sightings of Elvis or his ghost are common all over the world. Moreover, many people who visit Elvis's grave at his home Graceland in Memphis, Tennessee, seem more like worshipers on pilgrimage than fans.*

9 JANUARY

Plough Monday. *For farm laborers in rural England and Scotland, the first Monday after Epiphany marked the end of the Christmas holidays and the return to daily toil. In observance of the day, it became customary for workers to draw a plough—or plow—through the village streets and solicit donations to pay for further festivities. Frequently, threshers and reapers carrying their tools joined the Plough Monday procession, which included a ritual sweeping with brooms to drive away ghosts.*

10 JANUARY

Iroquois new year ritual. *See below.*

Iroquois Feast of Dreams

The Iroquois of eastern North America begin their new year with the Feast of Dreams. As part of the festivities, some tribe members rampage through their villages, attacking people and property. Their seemingly mad behavior is said to be triggered by dreams, and a victim's only escape is to guess the contents of those dreams.

The False Faces, so called because they wear elaborate masks *(right)* that distinguish them as the tribe's healing spirits, also participate in the feast. Two of them visit each home, first rubbing rattles along the frame.

11 JANUARY

Warding off witches. *In the Scottish town of Burghead, fishermen continue a once-common mysterious rite whose original purpose was likely to frighten away witches. At about dusk on January 11, the fishermen gather to assemble a Clavie—a barrel half-filled with tar and attached to a five-foot pole. Setting the tar afire, the fishermen carry the Clavie through the village and deposit it on top of a small mound. An assembled crowd watches the Clavie burn far into the night. Then the charred barrel is broken into pieces, which are seized by the townspeople as charms against witchcraft.*

12 JANUARY

Hindu solstice ritual. *In India, Hindus observe Makara-Sankranti, a solstice festival, by gathering to bathe in sacred rivers, particularly the Ganges. Singing joyous songs, they honor the approach of spring by coloring their food with saffron and wearing yellow clothes.*

13 JANUARY

Yodeling in the year. *Townspeople of Urnäsch in Switzerland, who still use the old Julian calendar, observe the last day of the year on Saint Silvester's Day, January 13. To celebrate, bands of well-wishers wearing elaborate costumes of sticks, moss, and other natural objects (above), wander through the countryside clanging bells to frighten off evil spirits. They yodel greetings at farmhouses along the way, where families present them with coins and mulled wine.*

14 JANUARY

Pongal Festival. *In the state of Tamil Nadu in southern India, the three-day Pongal Festival ushers in the new year, gives thanks for the rainy season, and celebrates the January rice harvest. Women cook the new rice in milk, and when it starts to bubble, they call out "Pongal!" ("It boils!") They then offer the sweet mixture to Surya, the Sun God. The festival's last day honors the cattle who help with harvesting. Farmers bedeck their cows with flowers and paint their horns, then lead them in a procession. After a feast that evening, men try to snatch bundles of money from the foreheads of fierce bulls (below).*

Upon entering, they extinguish the kitchen fire and scatter its ashes to ensure the health of the house's inhabitants. Then they dance to ceremonial songs, for which they are given tobacco; if they do not receive this gift, the False Faces may steal food from the kitchen cupboards.

The False Faces also dance in tribal long houses, where social and religious meetings are held. As part of the midwinter renewal of the tribe, they stir the ashes of the stove in the long house and blow them onto the bodies of the sick.

15 JANUARY

An alchemical feat. *When an alleged philosophers' stone (capable of transforming base metals into gold) was brought to his Prague court on this date in 1648, the Holy Roman Emperor Ferdinand III tested it himself. According to contemporary accounts, in each of two separate experiments he used a small portion of the stone to successfully convert two and a half pounds of mercury to gold. Ferdinand ordered a special medal struck to commemorate the "divine metamorphosis."*

16 JANUARY

Appeasing the fire god. *During this month in the Tengger Mountains of East Java, Indonesia, local Buddhists bring offerings to Betoro Bromo, the god of fire believed to live in Mount Bromo, an active volcano. As part of the celebration known as Kassada, thousands bearing food and flowers come on foot to the mountain; monks bless the gifts, then lead a procession up to the lip of the crater. At midnight, the pilgrims throw their offerings into the volcano to garner the blessings of the fiery god.*

17 JANUARY

Wassailing apple trees. *Villagers in Somerset, England, go wassailing on this date to serenade apple trees. The custom, dating back to Celtic Britain, includes shooting guns to ward off evil spirits, and singing songs (above), dancing, and pouring libations over tree roots to ensure fertility.*

18 JANUARY

Kitchen god. *At the end of the Chinese year, Zao Jun, the kitchen god (below), reports to the great Jade Emperor on everyone's actions. To curry favor, householders give the god sweet rice cakes, then pray as they burn a paper image of him. Children throw beans on the roof to simulate the sound of horses' hooves, and Zao Jun rides the smoke and flames to heaven.*

19 JANUARY

A mysterious well-wisher. *For many years, a stranger dressed in a black suit and hat and bearing gifts has visited the Baltimore grave of poet and author Edgar Allan Poe early in the morning on this date, the anniversary of the writer's birth. In 1990, an observer saw the mystery visitor place a half-full bottle of expensive French cognac and three red roses at the base of Poe's grave, then kneel as if in prayer. When he left, the stranger tipped his hat in the direction of the grave.*

20 JANUARY

An Irish holy man. *On this day Catholics remember Saint Feichin, a sixth-century Irish monk whose life is said to have been marked by many miracles. When he was a boy, Feichin's parents placed him in bed between them to sleep. Strangely, by morning he was often found lying on the floor with arms out-stretched, his body taking the shape of a cross; a bevy of angels report-edly hovered over his head. As an adult, Feichin is said to have caused a hostile king's fortress to sponta-neously burst into flames. He also purportedly brought a dead man to life and carried Jesus Christ—dis-guised as a leper—on his back.*

21 JANUARY

Saint Agnes Day. *In keeping with a long-standing tradition that has largely disappeared, English girls made special cakes on this day to honor Saint Agnes, who was put to death at age twelve for refusing to renounce Christianity in third-century Rome. After the cakes were baked, each girl walked upstairs backwards carrying one, then prayed to Saint Agnes. The ritual was intended to trigger a dream of the man the girl would marry.*

22 JANUARY

Mysterious measure of gold. *On this date in 1667, using a tincture left with him by a mysterious stranger, the Dutch physician John Friedrich Helvetius (above) is said to have transmuted a small quantity of lead into "the most excellent gold in the world." The enigmatic bearer of the tincture, who appeared to be a middle-aged Scotsman, told Helvetius that he had obtained it from a foreign occultist. He then began a demonstration in Helvetius's own laboratory, but departed before it was done, never to return. When Helvetius continued the experiment the next day, he produced a small measure of gold, but the means to make more was gone forever.*

Aquarius: January 20-February 18

Although winter snows may still blanket the earth, new growth is beginning in the soil tucked beneath when the zodiac arrives at Aquarius. In contrast to solitary, pragmatic Capricorns, natives of Aquarius are outgoing and idealistic. Like Capricorns, however, they value their independence, sometimes to the point of sacrificing intimate relationships.

The symbol of Aquarius is the Water Bearer, who pours water from a vast con-tainer—representing Aquarians' ability to disseminate new ideas. In fact, natives of this sign are often vitally committed to the spread of change and the betterment of society. Astrologers ascribe this to the influ-ence of the planet Uranus, which spurs Aquarians on to revolutionary acts that sometimes involve wild rebellion and even violence. Fortunately, Saturn, which also rules Aquarius, usually transforms such destructive impulses into effective activism.

Natives of Aquarius count among their gifts flexible, insightful thinking and clear-eyed rationality. These traits often produce great creativity, which Aquarians harness to worthy endeavors—the pursuit of high ideals, for instance, or the quest for technological innovation. Fired by vivid imaginations, Aquarians sometimes fall into thinking that their visions of a bright future for humanity are enough to make it so. When they learn to translate their ideals into reality, however, Aquarians can play important roles in help-ing to create a society that values the happi-ness and contributions of all its members. Famous Aquarians include sixteenth-century astronomer Galileo, dancer Mikhail Barysh-nikov, and actress Mia Farrow.

The Chinese New Year

The traditional Chinese New Year celebration was the year's gayest and most extravagant event. The festivities began on the second new moon after the winter solstice and continued for two weeks, until the full moon; during that time, many shops stayed closed and business ground to a halt.

The two-week hiatus was a welcome respite from the frenzied commercial activity of the previous month, when shops were filled with people buying holiday gifts. Since everyone tried to greet the new year with no outstanding debts, shopkeepers slashed prices during the last week of the year to earn cash to pay off creditors. Even the poorest families shopped for new shoes, since walking in old shoes on New Year's Day would bring bad luck.

On New Year's Eve, the shops were locked and the streets deserted. Families gathered behind doors sealed with strips of red paper—red being the color of luck—to keep out evil spirits. At midnight, family members ceremoniously kowtowed to the head of the house and his wife. Then gifts of coins in red envelopes were presented to the children, and everyone went to bed.

The first day of the new year was devoted to ancestor worship, and people were on their best behavior; bad luck would follow any shouting, lying, or cursing. Succeeding days were increasingly festive. Friends went visiting, bearing gifts; children sang for sweet rice cakes; and roaming musicians and actors performed the Dragon Play.

The final night of festivities was marked by the Lantern Festival *(see January 27)*, the main surviving feature of Chinese New Year celebrations. People festoon their houses and gardens with lanterns of all shapes and colors (except white, the color of mourning), and a dragon, the Chinese symbol of goodness and strength, winds its way through the streets. The paper beast is borne on the shoulders of men and boys hidden beneath it *(above)*. Watching crowds set off strings of firecrackers to bring the New Year's holiday to a riotous close.

23 JANUARY

A ghostly battle in the sky. *In the wee hours of this day in 1647, during the English Civil War, shepherds and travelers in Northamptonshire, England, described a strange phenomenon. They claimed to have seen in the sky an apparition of a battle that had been fought two months earlier between the forces of the king and those of Parliament. The vision faded but reappeared on and off over the next two weeks, each time accompanied by the sounds of war—clashing arms, solemn drumbeats, and the groans of the wounded. By the time the apparition disappeared for good, some witnesses could point out participants from the actual campaign in the celestial manifestation.*

24 JANUARY

Beloved peddler. *The Alacitas Fair in La Paz, Bolivia, honors not only the Virgin of La Paz, credited with helping Spanish conquerors win a great battle in 1781, but also Ekeko, the Aymara Indians' god of prosperity, for whom a fair was held on this day in ancient times. Figures of Ekeko, a potbellied peddler burdened with food and domestic articles, are sold at the fair. Ekeko can supposedly supply a home with everything the image carries, so a strong market exists for miniature goods ranging from tiny loaves of bread to diminutive newspapers—completely legible and sometimes carrying editorials on political issues Ekeko might be able to influence.*

25 JANUARY

Tet. *The Vietnamese New Year festival known as Tet is replete with good-luck rituals. Each family's kitchen god is said to ride to heaven on a carp's back; some households buy a carp (below) and release it on the festival's first day. Offerings are made to gods and ancestors to further ensure good fortune, and families take care that the year's first visitor does not have an inauspicious surname such as Meo (cat) or Cho (dog); guests named Tho (longevity) or Kim (gold) are warmly welcomed on this day.*

26 JANUARY

Turning the calendar in China. *See above.*

27 JANUARY

Lantern festival. *The culmination of the Chinese New Year celebration, the Lantern Festival, is variously said to have originated as a means to bid winter goodbye and welcome the increasing light and warmth of the sun, and as a fertility ceremony. All types of lanterns are displayed, and the more imaginative the lantern's form, the more prestige for the family who shows it. Some lanterns hold special significance: Those in the shape of little boys, for example, are often displayed by childless couples. Also on this day, families make offerings to ancestors and notify them of any sons born during the preceding year.*

28 JANUARY

Viking blaze. *Shetland Islanders celebrate their Viking heritage on the final Tuesday in January with the festival of Up-Helly-Aa. This last day of the traditional Yuletide climaxes with the burning of a thirty-foot replica of a Norse longship, which is escorted to the sea front by a platoon of men dressed as Vikings. Onlookers admire the ship until nightfall, then, in a ceremony evocative of an ancient Norse funeral, it is carried by torchlit procession to a field. There the torches are hurled into the ship, which explodes into flames (above). In earlier days, the festival officially ended at midnight with an exorcism of evil spirits from village homes.*

29 JANUARY

A mystic and a scholar. *Swedish scientist and mystic Emanuel Swedenborg (below) was born on this day in 1688. Distinguished as an astronomer, anatomist, and geologist, he devoted himself to religious work at the age of fifty-nine. Thereafter Swedenborg recounted conversations he had with angels and revelations that he said came directly from God—including detailed visions of heaven and hell.*

30 JANUARY

Celebration of planting. *The Feriae Sementiva, or Feast of Sowing, was the first of a long series of ancient Roman agricultural festivals intended to guarantee a favorable harvest. Sacrifices were made to Tellus, the earth, and Ceres, goddess of agriculture, as well as such minor deities as the gods of plowing, hoeing, and weeding. So concerned were the Romans that they might inadvertently overlook—and thus enrage—a god of tillage that they acknowledged in their prayers "any unknown god, male or female."*

In a gathering that honors the goddess Sarasvati, Nepalese officials crowd the courtyard at Hanuman Dhoka, an ancient palace in Katmandu, to join the king in rites of spring. Gun salutes praise the season, and the royal priest performs ceremonies of veneration.

31 JANUARY

In praise of learning. *In late January, Hindus in south Asia celebrate Basant Panchami in honor of Sarasvati, goddess of learning. The Katmandu valley of Nepal is crowded with students on this day, when Sarasvati is believed to pay an annual visit. In addition to bringing food, flowers, and incense to her temples, students offer Sarasvati pens, brushes, and books in the hope of help on their exams.*

1 FEBRUARY

Warding off fire and storm. *On this day, Ireland honors Saint Bridget, the patron saint of cattle and dairy farming. At one time, people made diamond-shaped Saint Bridget's crosses from straw to hang in homes or barns as protection against lightning and fire. In some regions, young people still fashion a "crios Bride" (Saint Bridget's girdle), a loop of straw rope with four crosses attached. Carrying it from house to house, they let neighbors pass through it to earn the saint's protection in the coming year.*

2 FEBRUARY

A day for candles. *In ancient Rome, Februalia festivals honored Demeter, who sought her daughter Persephone with lighted candles. In the Christian adaptation known as Candlemas, which takes place on this day, lighted candles are carried in procession to honor the Virgin Mary. Candlemas has long been a day for weather prediction—it is Groundhog Day in the United States—usually based on contraries. Sunny weather on Candlemas portends a late spring, while poor weather promises a bright spring and a temperate summer.*

3 FEBRUARY

Blessing of the Throats. *The patron of weavers, carvers, and builders, Saint Blaise was martyred on this day in AD 316. The saint was noted for his miraculous healing of a choking boy—a cure commemorated on his feast day with a ceremony known as the Blessing of the Throats, intended to ward off the throat ailments of winter.*

Brides in Their Beds

As the days grew longer after the darkness of winter, heralding the return of new life in the coming spring, the Celts celebrated a festival called Imbolc, honoring the Earth Mother Brigit. A protective guardian against the forces of darkness, Brigit, also known as Bride, was the goddess of both fire and fertility. To mark her special day, women made dolls from sheaves of corn or oats clothed in female attire, which were placed in special baskets called Bride's Beds *(right)*. As described above, Christians later adopted the holiday for Saint Bridget, patron of cattle and dairy farming.

Exorcising Winter in Japan

The festival known as Setsubun is a Japanese celebration of the exorcism of winter, intended to banish evil spirits in preparation for the arrival of spring. Householders walk through their homes scattering beans into all the corners to drive out any demons that lurk there *(right)*. To keep the devils away, they mount pointed branches and sardine heads above their doorways. The fish heads are said to repulse devils by their strong smell, and the branches are meant to poke out evil eyes. The beans, associated with good luck, are saved to be cooked and eaten after the first clap of spring thunder.

In temples and shrines throughout Japan, Setsubun occasions more formal purification rituals. One typical ceremony at a temple in the small country town of Ayabe expunges the sins of believers during an all-night vigil. Priests read from slips of paper called *hitogata,* on which are written the names of people who seek divine support.

After they are read, the hitogata are placed in special jars and carried to a bridge over an icy river. The priests empty the jars into the river in an avalanche of paper, and clumps of prayers begin to drift down the dark water to the ocean—and to the gods.

4 FEBRUARY

Setsubun: Driving winter away. *See above.*

5 FEBRUARY

Seismic sensitivity. *On this night in 1783, German poet Johann Wolfgang von Goethe (below) told his valet that tremors were shaking the earth. The servant was perplexed, since he felt no quakes, but the truth of his master's declaration was borne out two weeks later when news arrived from the Mediterranean: At the moment of Goethe's statement, a terrible quake had rocked Calabria and Sicily.*

6 FEBRUARY

A night in the snow. *For a few days at the beginning of February, children of northern Japan take part in a snow festival honoring the spirits that bring water to their island home. Miniature shrines are assembled in igloo-like huts, and, for one night, the children are permitted to wait out the darkness in these temporary shelters, receiving visits from parents and friends.*

7 FEBRUARY

A festival of new life. *As early spring arrives in China, countryfolk celebrate Li Chum, the very name of which means "Spring is here." The highlight of the day is a parade in which everyone marches. Some people carry small clay effigies of the water buffalo—a symbol of new life—while others bear an enormous likeness of the animal made from bamboo and colored paper. The procession makes its way to a temple, where the marchers smash the clay buffaloes and burn the bamboo-and-paper one. The spirit of the burning effigy is thought to climb to heaven to plead for a prosperous season.*

8 FEBRUARY

Thanks to the stars. *Shortly after the Chinese New Year, tradition-minded Chinese families celebrate the Star Festival, a nighttime ritual of thanks to the stars that influence human destiny. The master of the house offers a special prayer to the star that governed his birth, then lights 108 small lamps on a special altar. As the lamps burn out, each son of the household pays honor to his own star by relighting three of the lamps and judging from the brightness of the flames whether to expect good luck or bad luck in the days that follow.*

9 FEBRUARY

An eager martyr. *Today is the feast of Saint Apollonia, a third-century Egyptian deaconess. As an elderly woman, Apollonia was seized along with other Christians by a furious mob of unbelievers. They beat her jaws, breaking out all her teeth, and threatened to burn her alive unless she recanted her faith in Christ. Defiant, she refused and leaped into the already kindled flames before her attackers could further abuse her. Because of her broken teeth, Saint Apollonia is often depicted holding a tooth, and some Catholics pray to her when suffering dental problems.*

10 FEBRUARY

Hopes for good fishing. *The new year in Argungu, Nigeria, opens with a festival to mark the start of the fishing season. Thousands of members of the Kebbawa tribe line the banks of the Sokoto River, armed with large dippers and fishing nets. As the festival begins, everyone jumps into the river with a nearly simultaneous splash, hoping that fish startled by the commotion will leap into the nets. A prize goes to the person who catches the largest fish, but the overall size of the catch is also important, as an indication of the gods' sentiments toward the Kebbawa people.*

11 FEBRUARY

Healing the sick. *On this date in 1858, fourteen-year-old Bernadette Soubirous was collecting firewood near the town of Lourdes, France, when she saw a "beautiful lady" in the mouth of a grotto across a millstream. It was the first of eighteen visions of the Virgin Mary which gradually led Bernadette to a hidden spring inside the grotto. Pilgrims soon began bottling the spring water, which became renowned for its curative properties. Today millions of pilgrims like those above visit the shrine of Our Lady of Lourdes each year to worship and to seek miraculous cures for their ailments.*

12 FEBRUARY

Helping the crops grow. *When a new crescent moon appears at about this time, the Pueblo and Hopi peoples of the southwestern United States begin the lengthy Powamu festival by planting beans in the kivas—large buildings used for religious rituals. While the beans grow, as many as two hundred kachina dancers—ceremonial participants wearing masks representing the energy of the life force— perform rituals (below) to ensure a good crop. Meanwhile, children of the Pueblo and Hopi between the ages of six and ten are initiated into their kachina societies and given gifts by the dancers.*

13 FEBRUARY

Reverence for the dead. *During the week of February 13 to February 21, ancient Romans honored their dead, particularly their parents, during Parentalia, a festival commemorated in the above statue of a man holding busts of his ancestors. Temples were closed and marriages forbidden, while people visited ancestral tombs, leaving wine, milk, and flowers to placate family ghosts, who were thought to linger near the tombs and might otherwise haunt the living.*

14 FEBRUARY

Saint Valentine's Day. *See below.*

15 FEBRUARY

A bloody tradition. *On the Roman holiday of Lupercalia, a group of young noblemen gathered at the Lupercal, a cave believed to be the den of the wolf that suckled Romulus and Remus, the twin founders of Rome (above). After sacrificing goats and a dog, the men smeared themselves with blood, dressed in the animals' skins, then circled the old city slapping people with strips of goat skin. Women volunteered to be struck, to induce fertility and guarantee easy childbirth.*

Pairing Off on Valentine's Day

In the year AD 270, the Roman priest Valentine was martyred by the Emperor Claudius for secretly performing forbidden Christian marriages. The church later tied the pagan festival Lupercalia *(see February 15)* to Saint Valentine's feast day.

Since Victorian times, cards like the one at right have been sent to loved ones on Valentine's Day, a connection with romance that probably harks back to the Lupercalia custom of pairing couples by lot. After drawing names, young people exchanged gifts and stayed partners for the rest of the festival. Perhaps reinforced by the folk belief that birds choose their mates on February 14, the idea of Valentine's Day as a time for courtship grew in popularity through the Middle Ages. The day was also one for young women to divine their marriage prospects, by such means as watching for particular birds. A robin portended marriage to a sailor; a sparrow, a happy union with a poor man; a goldfinch, a wealthy husband.

Pisces: February 19-March 20

Pisces ends the cycle of the zodiac at about the same time that winter loses its icy grip upon all but the coldest climes. Streams and rivers swell with snowmelt—the waters of Pisces' ruler, Neptune.

Astrologers say that the Piscean symbol—two fish linked by a cord—indicates a duality inherent in the sign. For Pisces natives have the capacity not only to range far and wide in the world but also to plumb mystical depths. They tend to be emotional, intuitive, and vulnerable—traits that contribute to unworldly impracticality as well as passionate artistic expression.

Innate sensitivity makes Pisceans easily swayed by others, and some people born under the sign are so receptive to outside influences as to possess psychic powers. This gift of openness endows Pisceans with a radically different view of the world—at once a burden and a blessing. On the negative side, natives of Pisces may cease to function well in the rational world, leading a dreamy existence that is all too often enhanced by drugs or alcohol. More positively, however, the tendency to escape mundane consciousness may join forces with Pisceans' artistic creativity, finding outlets in startlingly beautiful poetry, dance, or theater.

Because Pisceans are visionaries, more attuned than most to the mystical underpinnings of life, they often have difficulty getting along with less spiritually inclined people. Nevertheless, their natural sympathy and kindness win them many friends and make it possible for them to convey their sense of wonder to the wider world. Some Pisceans who have succeeded in doing so are Renaissance sculptor Michelangelo, poet Elizabeth Browning, and novelist John Steinbeck.

16 FEBRUARY

Tibetan feats of daring. *Marked by shows, parades, and archery competitions, Losar, the Tibetan New Year, was once the greatest festival of the year. One event featured men sliding hundreds of feet down from the battlements of the Potala Palace in Lhasa on ropes made of yak hair—an attraction that was eventually ended when too many participants were injured. In the days preceding Losar, monks drove out the evil influences of the old year with a Devil Dance. Dressed in brilliant silks and huge, hideously painted masks, they danced for hours until a sorcerer succeeded with a spell against the demons.*

17 FEBRUARY

Dawn of the Kali Yuga. *On this date in 3102 BC, say Hindus, the world entered the Kali Yuga, the Evil Age, the last and most sinful of four great epochs. They believe the Kali Yuga, personified by the destroyer-goddess Kali (below), will endure for 432,000 years and end with the world's destruction. Then a new cycle of eras will begin with Krita Yuga, the Golden Age of truth.*

18 FEBRUARY

A glimpse of a sea serpent? *On this date in 1849, a Captain Adams and his crew aboard the vessel Lucy and Nancy got a brief look at what they took to be a strange, large, living animal off the coast of Florida. For unrecorded reasons their view of the supposed beast was obscured, but they reported seeing what they apparently thought was its extended neck and head above the surface as it moved through the water.*

19 FEBRUARY

The sun enters the sign of Pisces. *See above.*

20 FEBRUARY

Founding of the SPR. *See below.*

21 FEBRUARY

Feralia. *On this date in ancient Rome, Feralia—a kind of All Souls' Day— ended the week-long Parentalia festival. It was an occasion for family reunions and for the worship of Lares like the one pictured above. Lares were ancestral spirits believed to guard the home.*

22 FEBRUARY

An egg-shaped UFO. *On this day in 1979, two girls sledding near their home in West Yorkshire, England, were purportedly startled by a humming sound as red and green lights cast a glow on the snow. According to their later accounts of the episode, a gray, egg-shaped object roughly the size of a compact car landed on a nearby slope, then moved some yards to another location. Moments later it flew away, leaving depressions in the snow. Although nobody else observed the landing, another witness reported seeing a similar flying object some fifteen minutes before the girls' alleged encounter.*

23 FEBRUARY

Honoring boundaries. *Terminalia, the last festival of the old Roman year, honored Terminus, the god of boundaries and frontiers. Neighbors met where their fields adjoined to drape garlands on the stone boundary markers, or termini, and offer sacrifices of corn, honey, and wine. The stones were held to be sacred to Terminus, and anyone who moved them was accursed.*

Organizing the Study of Psychic Phenomena

On February 20, 1882, a group of prominent philosophers and physicists banded together with other interested people to found the Society for Psychical Research (SPR) in London. The purpose of the society was to support organized and systematic research into such "debatable phenomena" as telepathy, clairvoyance, and hauntings, with a view to determining their scientific basis, if any.

The establishment of the SPR raised research in the field to a new level, with an emphasis on controlled experiments like the one illustrated here. Even the group's trained scientists could not always detect hoaxes, however. During one experiment on thought-reading shortly after the group's founding, SPR investigators were taken in by a clever piece of stage magic employed by the popular hypnotist who was the subject of the study. Not until nearly thirty years later was the deception made known, when the hypnotist's partner published two articles that revealed the truth.

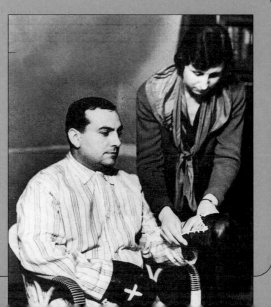

In a 1931 study, an SPR official fits Italian medium Pasquale Erto with boxing gloves to prevent cheating during a séance. Erto, nicknamed "the human rainbow" for the colored lights he produced in séances, was ultimately proved a fraud. He had drawn on his chemical training, not the spirit world, to create the dazzling effects.

Revelry Before the Solemn Fast

In some Catholic countries, the pre-Lenten Carnival is one of the year's most joyous celebrations. Although its timing is governed by the Church calendar, Carnival incorporates such pagan elements as the chaos of Saturnalia and the orgiastic rites that once heralded spring's arrival.

The name of the festival probably derived from *carne vale*—"farewell meat"—for the last meat eaten on Shrove Tuesday before the forty-day Lenten fast. But the word, like the festival itself, may have come from the Roman *car navale*, a type of cart that carried divine images in Roman parades.

Although Carnival's origins are unclear, by the Middle Ages it was established as a time for aristocratic tournaments and pageants. In later centuries, common folk took over the holiday, which culminated on Shrove Tuesday night when costumed revelers lighted candles and paraded through the streets seeking to blow out other candles while keeping their own burning.

Transported to the New World, Carnival found more extravagant expression. In New Orleans, Mardi Gras (Fat Tuesday) is a raucous festival. Social groups spend thousands of hours and small fortunes creating gorgeous floats for the parade, in which costumed dancers cavort to the music of jazz bands.

The grandest Carnival celebration, however, takes place in Rio de Janeiro, Brazil, where it marks the onset of the Southern Hemisphere's autumn. Introduced by early settlers, Carnival began as a rude explosion of merriment that saw pranksters pelting pedestrians with oranges and eggs. It evolved into four days of elegant balls, elaborate masquerades, and energetic dancing. Groups called samba schools join in a parade, competing for prizes with their fantastic costumes, spectacular floats, and impeccably rehearsed music and dancing. The samba schools offer fleeting fame to Rio's poorest citizens, whose meager savings underwrite much of the flamboyance of Carnival.

In stiff competition with his car for most garish costume, the Mardi Gras reveler above drives a parade route in New Orleans. At right, a dazzling float makes its way through Rio de Janeiro at Carnival.

24 FEBRUARY

Shiva's Night. *At about this time, devout Hindus observe a holiday known as Shivaratri, literally Shiva's Night, a vigil that honors the many-faceted god of destruction and renewal (below). After a day of total fasting, without even a drink of water, believers gather at Shiva shrines, where they stay awake all night watching the flames of small oil lamps.*

25 FEBRUARY

Carnival! *See above.*

26 FEBRUARY

Penitential ashes. *Just after Carnival comes Ash Wednesday, the first day of a forty-day period of abstinence called Lent meant to prepare worshipers for the solemn rites of Easter. The name of the day comes from the custom of sprinkling the head with ashes as a symbol of penance; the ashes were said to come from the burning of Christmas greenery or a Yule log. Today the ceremonial ash is administered by a priest at a Lenten mass, by pressing his ash-covered thumb to each person's forehead.*

27 FEBRUARY

Death of an immortal. *The Comte de Saint Germain, who claimed he had lived for centuries and known the Queen of Sheba, allegedly died on this date in 1784—although some say he was seen alive in the 1900s.*

Birth of a visionary. *Austrian psychic and philosopher Rudolf Steiner (below), founder of anthroposophy, was born this day in 1861. Steiner devised new methods of farming, education, painting, and architecture to help others achieve personal experience of the spiritual.*

28 FEBRUARY

Mourning for a martyr. *Among Shi'ite Muslims, this first day of the month of Muharram begins a ten-day festival commemorating the death of Hussain, the martyred grandson of Muhammad. For nine days the faithful gather in Karbala, Iraq, to hear orators tell the story of Hussain and his followers. On the tenth day, processions fill the streets, and some scourge themselves (below) to recall Hussain's suffering.*

29 FEBRUARY

Leap Day. *To keep his Western calendar in line with the solar year, Julius Caesar decreed that every fourth year would include an extra day, February 29. By tradition, leap year is a time for women to propose marriage to men, a custom formalized in 1288 by the Scottish Parliament, which declared that any "maiden lady of both high and low estate shall have liberty to bespeak the man she like."*

ACKNOWLEDGMENTS

The editors wish to thank the following for their assistance: Dr. John Carlson, University of Maryland, Silver Spring; Instituto Archeologico Germanico, Rome; Jeffery Jerome, Edgar Allan Poe House, Baltimore; Donatien Laurent, Directeur de Recherche au CNRS, Brest, France; Patricia A. Paterno, First Impression, McLean, Virginia.

BIBLIOGRAPHY

Adderley, James Granville, *St. Francis of Assisi and His Friends.* London: Edward Arnold, 1901.

Alexander, Marc, *British Folklore.* New York: Crescent Books, 1982.

Ancient Wisdom and Secret Sects. (Mysteries of the Unknown series.) Alexandria, Va.: Time-Life Books, 1989.

Anderson, Mary M., *The Festivals of Nepal.* London: George Allen & Unwin, 1971.

Art of the Abelam: New Guinea. Long Beach: California State University, 1975.

Arthur, Mildred H., *Holidays of Legend.* Irvington-on-Hudson, N.Y.: Harvey House, no date.

Attenborough, David, *Journeys to the Past.* Guildford, Surrey, England: Lutterworth Press, 1981.

Bass, Catriona, *Inside the Treasure House.* London: Victor Gollancz, 1990.

Bauer, Helen, and Sherwin Carlquist, *Japanese Festivals.* Garden City, N.Y.: Doubleday, 1965.

Berns, Marla, *Àgbáyé: Yoruba Art in Context.* Exhibition catalog. Los Angeles: UCLA Museum of Cultural History, 1979.

Bjornsson, Arni, *Islandic Feasts and Holidays,* 1980.

Bord, Janet, and Colin Bord, *Earth Rites.* London: Granada, 1982.

Brennan, Martin, *The Stars and the Stones.* London: Thames and Hudson, 1983.

Brookesmith, Peter, *The UFO Casebook.* New York: Warner Books, 1989.

Burland, C. A., *Echoes of Magic.* Totowa, N.J.: Rowman and Littlefield, 1972.

Campanelli, Pauline, *Wheel of the Year.* St. Paul: Llewellyn, 1989.

Campbell, Joseph, *The Masks of God: Primitive Mythology.* New York: Penquin Books, 1969.

Carlson, John B., "America's Ancient Skywatchers." *National Geographic,* March 1990.

Cavendish, Richard, ed., *Man, Myth & Magic.* New York: Marshall Cavendish, 1985.

Celebration: A World of Art and Ritual. Exhibition catalog. Washington, D.C.: Smithsonian Institution, 1982.

Chambers, Kevin, *The Travelers' Guide to Asian Customs & Manners.* Deephaven, Minn.: Meadowbrook, 1988.

Chase's Annual Events: Special Days, Weeks & Months in 1991. Chicago: Contemporary Books, 1991.

Clendinnen, Inga, "The Cost of Courage in Aztec Society." *Past & Present,* May 1985.

Comets, Asteroids, and Meteorites. (Voyage Through the Universe series.) Alexandria, Va.: Time-Life Books, 1990.

Cooper, Gordon, *Festivals of Europe.* London: Percival Marshall, 1961.

Cooper, J. C., *The Aquarian Dictionary of Festivals.* Wellingborough, Northamptonshire, England: Aquarian Press, 1990.

Cosmic Connections. (Mysteries of the Unknown series.) Alexandria, Va.: Time-Life Books, 1988.

Couzens, Reginald C., *The Stories of the Months and Days.* Detroit: Gale Research, 1970 (reprint of 1923 edition).

Crumrine, N. Ross, and Marjorie Halpin, eds., *The Power of Symbols.* Vancouver: University of British Columbia Press, 1983.

Daniels, Cora Linn, and C. M. Stevans, eds., *Encyclopaedia of Superstitions, Folklore, and the Occult Sciences of the World* (Vols. 1 and 3). Detroit: Gale Research, 1971 (reprint of 1903 edition).

Delgado, Pat, and Colin Andrews, *Circular Evidence.* London: Bloomsbury, 1989.

Dorcy, Mary Jean, *Shrines of Our Lady.* New York: Sheed and Ward, 1956.

Dreams and Dreaming. (Mysteries of the Unknown series.) Alexandria, Va.: Time-Life Books, 1990.

Drury, Nevill, *Dictionary of Mysticism and the Occult.* New York: Harper & Row, 1985.

Eberhard, Wolfram, *Chinese Festivals.* New York: Henry Schuman, 1952.

Eliade, Mircea:
The Myth of the Eternal Return, or Cosmos and History. Transl. by Willard R. Trask. Princeton, N.J.: Princeton University Press, 1954.
Patterns in Comparative Religion. Transl. by Rosemary Sheed. New York: New American Library, 1974.
The Sacred and the Profane. Transl. by Willard R. Trask. San Diego: Harcourt Brace Jovanovich, 1959.

The Far Planets. (Voyage Through the Universe series.) Alexandria, Va.: Time-Life Books, 1990.

Frazer, James George, *The Illustrated Golden Bough.* Garden City, N.Y.: Doubleday, 1978.

Freedman, Maurice, ed., *Social Organization: Essays Presented to Raymond Firth.* Chicago: Aldine, 1967.

Gaer, Joseph, *Holidays around the World.* Boston: Little, Brown, 1953.

Gault, Frank, and Claire Gault, *Stories from the Olympics.* New York: Walker, 1976.

Gauquelin, Michel, *Dreams and Illusions of Astrology.* Buffalo: Prometheus, 1979.

Gillett, Henry Martin, *Famous Shrines of Our Lady.* London: Samuel Walker, 1949.

Gillison, Gillian, "Living Theater in New Guinea's Highlands." *National Geographic,* August 1983.

Gonzalez-Wippler, Migene, *The Complete Book of Spells, Ceremonies and Magic.* St. Paul: Llewellyn, 1988.

Grant, James, *The Mysteries of All Nations: Rise and Progress of Superstition, Laws against and Trials of Witches, Ancient and Modern Delusions.* Detroit: Gale Research, 1971 (reprint of 1880 edition).

Green, Miranda, *The Gods of the Celts.* Totowa, N.J.: Barnes and Noble, 1986.

Hamlyn, Paul, *Roman Mythology.* London: Hamlyn, 1969.

Hass, Ernst, and Gisela Minke, *Himalayan Pilgrimage.* New York: Viking Press, 1978.

Hauntings. (Mysteries of the Unknown series.) Alexandria, Va.: Time-Life Books, 1989.

Hawthorn, Audrey, *Kwakiutl Art.* Seattle: University of Washington Press, 1988.

Henry, Bill, *History of the Olympic Games.* New York: G. P. Putnam's Sons, 1948.

Hieronimus, Robert, *The Two Great Seals of America.* Baltimore: Savitriaum, 1976.

James, E. O., *Seasonal Feasts and Festivals.* London: Thames and Hudson, 1961.

Jonaitis, Aldona, *From the Land of the Totem Poles.* Exhibition catalog. New York: American Museum of Natural History, 1988.

Joy, Margaret, *Days, Weeks and Months.* London: Faber and Faber, 1984.

Keegan, M. K., and Frontier Photographers, *Enduring Culture: A Century of Photography of the Southwest Indians.* Santa Fe, N.M.: Clear Light, 1990.

Kelley, Ruth Edna, *The Book of Hallowe'en.* Boston: Lothrop, Lee & Shepard, 1919.

Kelley, Thomas L., and Patricia Roberts, *Kathmandu: City on the Edge of the World.* New York: Abbeville Press, 1989.

Keuls, Eva C., *The Reign of the Phallus.* New York: Harper & Row, 1985.

Kightly, Charles, *The Customs and Ceremonies of Britain.* London: Thames and Hudson, 1986.

Krupp, E. C.:
Beyond the Blue Horizon. New York: Harper Collins, 1991.
Echoes of the Ancient Skies. New York: Harper & Row, 1983.

Latsch, Marie-Luise, *Chinese Traditional Festivals.* Beijing: New World Press, 1984.

Lee, Douglas, "Day of the Rice God." *National Geographic,* July 1978.

Levey, Judith S., and Agnes Greenhall, eds., *The Concise Columbia Encyclopedia.* New York: Columbia University Press, 1983.

Life Search. (Voyage Through the Universe series.) Alexandria, Va.: Time-Life Books, 1988.

Linton, Ralph, and Adelin Linton, *Halloween through Twenty Centuries.* New York: Henry Schuman, 1950.

Lyttleton, Margaret, and Werner Forman, *The Romans: Their Gods and Their Beliefs.* London: Orbis, 1984.

McDowell, Bart, and James P. Blair, "Orissa: Past and Promise in an Indian State." *National Geographic,* October 1970.

MacNeill, Máire, *The Festival of Lughnasa.* London: Oxford University Press, 1962.

Magical Arts. (Mysteries of the Unknown series.) Alexandria, Va.: Time-Life Books, 1990.

Mails, Thomas E., *Secret Native American Pathways: A Guide to Inner Peace.* Tulsa: Council Oak Books, 1988.

Majupuria, Trilok Chandra, and S. P. Gupta, *Nepal: The Land of Festivals.* New Delhi: S. Chand, 1981.

Markham, Ursula, *Fortune-Telling by Crystals and Semiprecious Stones.* Wellingborough, Northamptonshire, England: Aquarian Press, 1987.

Megas, George A., *Greek Calendar Customs.* Athens: Press and Information Department, Prime Minister's Office, 1958.

Miles, Clement A., *Christmas in Ritual and Tradition, Christian and Pagan.* Detroit: Omnigraphics, 1990 (reprint of 1912 edition).

Milne, Jean, *Fiesta Time in Latin America.* Los Angeles: Ward Ritchie Press, 1965.

Mullin, Redmond, *Miracles and Magic: The Miracles and Spells of Saints and Witches.* London: Mowbray, 1979.

Mysterious Creatures. (Mysteries of the Unknown series.) Alexandria, Va.: Time-Life Books, 1988.

Mysterious Lands and Peoples. (Mysteries of the Unknown series.) Alexandria, Va.: Time-Life Books, 1991.

Mystical Rites and Rituals. London: Octopus Books, 1975.

Mythes et Croyances du Monde Entier. Paris: Lidis-Brepols, 1985.

Nature: A Weekly Illustrated Journal of Science. (Supplement to *Nature* June 16, 1898.) November 1897 to April 1898. New York: Macmillan, 1898.

Nelson, Richard K., *Hunters of the Northern Ice.* Chicago: University of Chicago Press, 1969.

The New Catholic Encyclopedia. New York: McGraw Hill, 1967.

Palmer, Geoffrey, and Noel Lloyd, *A Year of Festivals.* London: Frederick Warne, 1972.

Patten, Helen Philbrook, *The Year's Festivals*. Boston: Dana Estes, 1903.

Phantom Encounters. (Mysteries of the Unknown series.) Alexandria, Va.: Time-Life Books, 1988.

Pieper, Josef, *In Tune with the World.* Transl. by Richard Winston and Clara Winston. New York: Harcourt, Brace & World, 1965.

Pike, Royston, *Round the Year with the World's Religions.* New York: Henry Schuman, 1951.

Powers of Healing. (Mysteries of the Unknown series.) Alexandria, Va.: Time-Life Books, 1989.

Price, Nancy, *Pagan's Progress: High Days and Holy Days.* London: Museum Press, 1954.

Rosen, Mike:
    Autumn Festivals. East Sussex, England: Wayland, 1990.
    Summer Festivals. East Sussex, England: Wayland, 1990.
    Winter Festivals. East Sussex, England: Wayland, 1990.

Ross, Anne, *The Pagan Celts.* London: B. T. Batsford, 1986.

Russell, Jeffrey B.:
    A History of Witchcraft. London: Thames and Hudson, 1980.
    Witchcraft in the Middle Ages. Secaucus, N.J.: Citadel Press, 1972.

Search for the Soul. (Mysteries of the Unknown series.) Alexandria, Va.: Time-Life Books, 1989.

Secrets of the Alchemists. (Mysteries of the Unknown series.) Alexandria, Va.: Time-Life Books, 1990.

Seymour, Percy, *Astrology: The Evidence of Science.* Luton, Beds, England: Lennard, 1988.

Shellabarger, Samuel, *Lord Chesterfield.* London: Mac-

Millan, 1935.

Shepard, Leslie, ed., *Encyclopedia of Occultism & Parapsychology.* Vol. 1. Detroit: Gale Research, 1991.

Smilgis, Martha, "A New Age Dawning." *Time,* August 31, 1987.

Snelling, John, *Buddhist Festivals.* Vero Beach, Fla.: Rourke Enterprises, 1987.

Speck, W. A., *Days, Weeks & Months.* Boston: Harvard University Press, 1977.

Spence, Lewis, *The Mysteries of Britain.* London: Rider, 1928.

Spencer, Robert F., *The North Alaskan Eskimo* (Bureau of American Ethnology, Bulletin 171). Washington, D.C.: Smithsonian Institution Press, 1969.

Spirit Summonings. (Mysteries of the Unknown series.) Alexandria, Va.: Time-Life Books, 1989.

Stein, Diane:
    Casting the Circle. Freedom, Calif.: Crossing Press, 1990.
    The Goddess Book of Days. St. Paul: Llewellyn, 1989.

van Straalen, Alice, *The Book of Holidays around the World.* New York: E. P. Dutton, 1986.

Tanabe, George J., Jr., and Willa Jane Tanabe, eds., *The Lotus Sutra in Japanese Culture.* Honolulu: University of Hawaii Press, 1989.

Thomas, P., *Epics, Myths and Legends of India.* Bombay: D. B. Taraporevala Sons, 1942.

Thukral, Gurmeet, and Arun Sanon, *Festive India.* New Delhi: Frank Bros., 1987.

Thurston, Herbert, *The Physical Phenomena of Mysticism.* Ed. by J. H. Crehan. London: Burns Oates, 1952.

Time and Space. (Mysteries of the Unknown series.) Alex-

andria, Va.: Time-Life Books, 1990.

Transactions of the Wisconsin Academy of Sciences, Arts, and Letters (Vol. 15, Part 2). Madison, Wisc.: Democrat Printing, 1907.

Turner, Victor, ed., *Celebration: Studies in Festivity and Ritual.* Washington, D.C.: Smithsonian Institution Press, 1982.

The UFO Phenomenon. (Mysteries of the Unknown series.) Alexandria, Va.: Time-Life Books, 1987.

Vermaseren, Maarten J., *Cybele and Attis: The Myth and the Cult.* Transl. by A. M. H. Lemmers. London: Thames and Hudson, 1977.

Vickery, A. R., *Holy Thorn of Glastonbury.* Guernsey, U.K.: Toucan Press, 1990.

Visions and Prophecies. (Mysteries of the Unknown series.) Alexandria, Va.: Time-Life Books, 1988.

Walsh, William S., *Curiosities of Popular Customs.* Detroit: Gale Research, 1966 (reprint of 1898 edition).

Whitlock, Ralph:
    A Calendar of Country Customs. London: B. T. Batsford, 1978.
    Thanksgiving and Harvest. Vero Beach, Fla.: Rourke Enterprises, 1987.

Wilson, P. W., *The Romance of the Calendar.* New York: W. W. Norton, no date.

Witches and Witchcraft. (Mysteries of the Unknown series.) Alexandria, Va.: Time-Life Books, 1990.

Wong, C. S., *An Illustrated Cycle of Chinese Festivities in Malaysia and Singapore.* Singapore: Jack Chia, 1987.

Wright, Paul, *The Literary Zodiac.* Edinburgh: Anodyne, 1987.

PICTURE CREDITS

The sources for the illustrations in this book are shown below. Credits from left to right are separated by semicolons; credits from top to bottom are separated by dashes.

Holford, Loughton, Essex. 74: © Erich Lessing, Vienna. 75: Werner Forman Archive, London/Museum für Volkerkunde, Basel. 76, 77: Ceremony and Magic: The North Alaskan Eskimo Whale Cult, courtesy the National Museum of Natural History, Smithsonian Institution, Washington, D.C., from the Smithsonian Institution exhibition "Crossroads of Continents: Cultures of Siberia and Alaska." 78, 79: Smithsonian Institution, slide no. 80 15613; trans. no. 3834, Steve Myers, courtesy Department of Library Services, American Museum of Natural History, New York. 80: Museum für Volkerkunde, Munich. 81: The Natural History Museum, London. 82, 83: Bill Hess/© National Geographic Society—British Library, London; Information Services Department, Accra, Ghana; Gurmeet Thukral, Mussoorie, India. 84, 85: Fortean Picture Library, Clwyd, Wales; Peter Clayton, Hemel Hempstead, Hertfordshire—Archives, Theosophical Society in America, Wheaton, Ill.; Homer Sykes, London. 86: Fortean Picture Library, Clwyd, Wales; Images Colour Library, Leeds, West Yorkshire—Alinari/Art Resource, New York. 87: Tony Morrison, South American Pictures, Woodbridge, Suffolk. 88: Bodleian Library, Oxford—Michael Holford, Loughton, Essex. 89: Mary Evans Picture Library, London—Michael Holford, Loughton, Essex. 90: Royal Geographical Society, London—The Bettmann Archive, New York; © Wolfgang Lauter, Munich. 91: © Thomas L. Kelly, New York. 92: Anne Marie Jauss, from Holidays Around the World by Joseph Gaer, Little, Brown and Company, Boston, 1953; Fortean Picture Library, Clwyd, Wales. 93: Syndication International, London—Fortean Picture Library, Clwyd, Wales. 94, 95: Bodleian Library, Oxford—Popperfoto, London; Topham Picture Source, Edenbridge, Kent; Haga Library, Tokyo. 96, 97: © John Dommer, Photo Researchers, New York; Peter Newark's Historical Pictures, Bath, Avon—AP/Wide World Photos, New York (2); Culver Pictures, New York. 98: Victor Englebert, Cali, Colombia. 99: Collections/Brian Shuel, London; Mansell Collection, London—Leif Geiges, Staufen, Germany. 100: Fortean Picture Library, Clwyd, Wales—Office National du Tourisme Thailandais. 101: Mangla Sharda, New York—Haga Library, Tokyo. 102: UPI/Bettmann, New York. 103: Bodleian Library, Oxford—Haga Library, Tokyo. 104, 105: © Joe Viesti/Viesti Associates, Inc., New York; Topham Picture Source, Edenbridge, Kent; Mansell Collection, London—line art by Time-Life Books; Bibliothèque Nationale, Paris. 106, 107: Trans. no. 2464(2), photo by Lee Boltin, courtesy Department of Library Services, American Museum of Natural History; Gurmeet Thukral, Mussoorie, India—© Ernst Haas, New York. 108, 109: © Neil Cooper/Panos Pictures, London. 110, 111: © Ernst Haas, New York; © Neil Cooper/Panos Pictures, London. 112: © Thomas L. Kelly, New York. 113: The Natural History Museum, London. 114, 115: Bildagentur Schapowalow, Hamburg; Office du Tourisme Turc, Paris—© R. Ian Lloyd, Singapore; UPI/Bettmann, New York. 116, 117: Vetten/Netherlands Board of Tourism, New York; Smithsonian Institution, National Museum of Natural History; © R. Rowen/Photo Researchers, New York—Michael Holford, Loughton, Essex; Erich Hartmann/Magnum Photos, Inc., New York. 118, 119: Biblioteca Governativa Di Lucca, courtesy Buch-und Kunsthandlung St. Hildegard, Rüdesheim; Bodleian Library, London—Linda Fisk, San Diego Museum of Man, San Diego, Calif.; Scala, Florence, courtesy Museo dell Opera del Duomo, Florence. 120: © 1985 Nathan Benn/Woodfin Camp Inc., Washington, D.C.—Steve McCurry/ © National Geographic Society; Photri, Falls Church, Va. 121: Scala, Florence, courtesy Musei Vaticani, Rome—Walter Körber, St. Petri-Dom, Schleswig. 122, 123: Michael Holford—Haga Library, Tokyo; UPI, New York; K. C. Den-Dooven, from Southwestern Indian Ceremonies by Tom Bahti, KC Publications, Las Vegas, Nev., 1970; SNS Pressebild, Innsbruck. 124, 125: UPI/Bettmann, New York; Joe Viesti/Viesti Associates, Inc., New York—National Museum of the American Indian, New York; Morihiro Oki, Tokyo. 126, 127: Collections/Brian Shuel, London; The Royal College of Physicians of London—© 1987 Ronni Pinsler, from An Illustrated Cycle of Chinese Festivities in Malaysia and Singapore by C. S. Wong, Malaysia Publishing House, Singapore, 1987; Bodleian Library, Oxford. 128, 129: Suzanne & Nick Geary/Tony Stone Worldwide, Chicago, Ill.; Collections/Brian Shuel, London—Hans Reinhard/Bruce Coleman Ltd.; Mary Evans Picture Library, London. 130: © Thomas L. Kelly, New York—Dan Campanelli, from Wheel of the Year—Living the Magical Life by Pauline Campanelli, Llewellyn Publications, St. Paul, Minn., 1989. 131: Sekai Bunka Photo, Tokyo—Hulton Picture Company, London. 132, 133: Gerard Guy/Camera Press, London; Alinari, Florence, courtesy Musei Capitolini, Rome; Scala, Florence, courtesy Musei Capitolini, Rome—photo no. 1824-D, Smithsonian Institution; Private collection. 134: Bodleian Library, Oxford—Zul/Chapel Studios, Hove, East Sussex. 135: Michael Holford, Loughton, Essex—Harry Price Library/Mary Evans Picture Library, London. 136, 137: Topham Picture Source; John Starr/Tony Stone Worldwide, Chicago, Ill.—Gurmeet Thukral, Mussoorie, India; Archiv für Kunst und Geschichte, Berlin; © Sipa-Press, New York.

Index

TIME-LIFE BOOKS

EDITOR-IN-CHIEF: Thomas H. Flaherty

Director of Editorial Resources: Elise D. Ritter-Clough
Executive Art Director: Ellen Robling
Director of Photography and Research: John Conrad Weiser
Editorial Board: Dale M. Brown, Janet Cave, Roberta
Conlan, Robert Doyle, Laura Foreman, Jim Hicks, Rita
Thievon Mullin, Henry Woodhead
Assistant Director of Editorial Resources: Norma E. Shaw

PRESIDENT: John D. Hall

Vice President and Director of Marketing: Nancy K. Jones
Editorial Director: Russell B. Adams, Jr.
Director of Production Services: Robert N. Carr
Production Manager: Prudence G. Harris
Director of Technology: Eileen Bradley
Supervisor of Quality Control: James King

Editorial Operations
Production: Celia Beattie
Library: Louise D. Forstall
Computer Composition: Deborah G. Tait (Manager),
Monika D. Thayer, Janet Barnes Syring, Lillian Daniels
Interactive Media Specialist: Patti H. Cass

Time-Life Books is a division of Time Life Incorporated

PRESIDENT AND CEO: John M. Fahey, Jr.

Library of Congress Cataloging in Publication Data
The Mystical Year / by the editors of Time-Life Books.
  p. cm.—(Mysteries of the unknown)
Includes bibliographical references and index.
ISBN 0-8094-6537-X
ISBN 0-8094-6538-8 (library)
1. Fasts and Feasts. 2. Religious calendars.
I. Time-Life Books.   II. Series.
BL590.M97 1992
291.3'6—dc20   91-42780
                                           CIP

MYSTERIES OF THE UNKNOWN

SERIES EDITOR: Jim Hicks
Series Administrator: Jane A. Martin
Art Directors: Ellen Robling (principal), Robert K. Herndon
Picture Editor: Susan V. Kelly

Editorial Staff for *The Mystical Year*
Text Editors: Robert Doyle (principal), Janet Cave, Roberta
Conlan, Esther Ferington
Associate Editors/Research: Denise Dersin (principal),
Gwen Mullen, Robert H. Wooldridge, Jr.
Assistant Art Directors: Susan M. Gibas, Brook Mowrey
Writer: Sarah D. Ince
Copy Coordinators: Donna Carey, Juli Duncan
Picture Coordinator: Julia Kendrick
Editorial Assistant: Donna Fountain

Special Contributors: Martha Lee Beckington, Thomas A.
DiGiovanni, Barbara Fleming, Patricia A. Paterno, Evelyn
S. Prettyman, Nancy J. Seeger, Priscilla Tucker (research);
Margery A. duMond, Marfé Ferguson Delano, Donal Kevin
Gordon, Lydia Preston Hicks, Susan Perry, Peter W.
Pocock, Robert H. White (text); John Drummond (design);
Hazel Blumberg-McKee (index).

Correspondents: Elisabeth Kraemer-Singh (Bonn); Christine
Hinze (London); Christina Lieberman (New York); Maria
Vincenza Aloisi (Paris); Ann Natanson (Rome); Dick Berry
(Tokyo). Valuable assistance was also provided by Mah-
met Ali Kislali (Ankara); Pavle Svabic (Belgrade); Angelika
Lemmer (Bonn); Judy Aspinall, Sarah Moule (London);
Trini Bandrés (Madrid); Meenakshi Ganguly (New Delhi);
Elizabeth Brown, Katheryn White (New York); Leonora
Dodsworth (Rome); Traudl Lessing (Vienna).

Other Publications:

WEIGHT WATCHERS® SMART CHOICE
  RECIPE COLLECTION
TRUE CRIME
THE AMERICAN INDIANS
THE ART OF WOODWORKING
LOST CIVILIZATIONS
ECHOES OF GLORY
THE NEW FACE OF WAR
HOW THINGS WORK
WINGS OF WAR
CREATIVE EVERYDAY COOKING
COLLECTOR'S LIBRARY OF THE UNKNOWN
CLASSICS OF WORLD WAR II
TIME-LIFE LIBRARY OF CURIOUS AND UNUSUAL FACTS
AMERICAN COUNTRY
VOYAGE THROUGH THE UNIVERSE
THE THIRD REICH
THE TIME-LIFE GARDENER'S GUIDE
TIME FRAME
FIX IT YOURSELF
FITNESS, HEALTH & NUTRITION
SUCCESSFUL PARENTING
HEALTHY HOME COOKING
UNDERSTANDING COMPUTERS
LIBRARY OF NATIONS
THE ENCHANTED WORLD
THE KODAK LIBRARY OF CREATIVE PHOTOGRAPHY
GREAT MEALS IN MINUTES
THE CIVIL WAR
PLANET EARTH
COLLECTOR'S LIBRARY OF THE CIVIL WAR
THE EPIC OF FLIGHT
THE GOOD COOK
WORLD WAR II
HOME REPAIR AND IMPROVEMENT
THE OLD WEST

*For information on and a full description of any of the Time-
Life Books series listed above, please call 1-800-621-7026
or write:*
Reader Information
Time-Life Customer Service
P.O. Box C-32068
Richmond, Virginia 23261-2068

This volume is one of a series that examines the history
and nature of seemingly paranormal phenomena. Other
books in the series include:

Mystic Places	*Witches and Witchcraft*
Psychic Powers	*Time and Space*
The UFO Phenomenon	*Magical Arts*
Psychic Voyages	*Utopian Visions*
Phantom Encounters	*Secrets of the Alchemists*
Visions and Prophecies	*Eastern Mysteries*
Mysterious Creatures	*Earth Energies*
Mind over Matter	*Cosmic Duality*
Cosmic Connections	*Mysterious Lands and Peoples*
Spirit Summonings	*The Mind and Beyond*
Ancient Wisdom	*Mystic Quests*
and Secret Sects	*Search for Immortality*
Hauntings	*The Psychics*
Powers of Healing	*Alien Encounters*
Search for the Soul	*The Mysterious World*
Transformations	*Master Index*
Dreams and Dreaming	*and Illustrated Symbols*